PROJECT APPRAISAL AND ANALYSIS

UNIT I

Introduction

Projects have a major role to play in the economic development of a country. Since the introduction of planning in our economy, we have been investing large amount of money in projects related to industry, minerals, power, transportation, irrigation, education etc. with a view to improve the socio-economic conditions of the people. These projects are designed with the aim of efficient management, earning adequate return to provide for future development with their own resources. But experience shows that there are several shortcomings in the ultimate success of achieving the objectives of the proposed project.

CONCEPT OF PROJECT AND PROJECT MANAGEMENT

The term project has a wider meaning. A project is accomplished by performing a set of activities. For example, construction of a house is a project. The construction of a house consists of many activities like digging of foundation pits, construction of foundation, construction of walls, construction of roof, fixing of doors and windows, fixing of sanitary fitting, wiring etc. Another aspect of project is the non-routine nature of activities. Each project is unique in the sense that the activities of a project are unique and non routine. A project consumes resources. The resources required for completing a project are men, material, money and time. Thus, we can define a project as an organized programme of pre-determined group of activities that are non-routine in nature and that must be completed using the available resources within the given time limit. Let us now consider some definitions of 'project'. Newman et. al define that "a project typically has a distinct mission that it is designed to achieve and a clear termination point the achievement of the mission".Gillinger defines "project" as the whole complex of activities involved in using resources to gain benefits. Project management institute, USA defined project as "a system involving the co-ordination of a number of separate department entities throughout organization, in a way it must be completed with prescribed schedules and time constraints".

According to the encyclopedia of management, *"project is an organized unit dedicated to the attainment of goal, the successful completion of a development project on time, within budget, in conformance with predetermined programme specification."*

Project management is an organised venture for managing projects, involves scientific application of modern tools and techniques in planning, financing, implementing, monitoring, controlling and coordinating unique activities or task produce desirable outputs in accordance with the determined objectives with in the constraints of time and cost.

CHARACTERISTICS OF PROJECT

(1) Objectives : A project has a set of objectives or a mission. Once the objectives are achieved the project is treated as completed.

(2) Life cycle : A project has a life cycle. The life cycle consists of five stages i.e. conception stage, definition stage, planning & organising stage, implementation stage and commissioning stage.

(3) Uniqueness : Every project is unique and no two projects are similar. Setting up a cement plant and construction of a highway are two different projects having unique features.

(4) Team Work : Project is a team work and it normally consists of diverse areas. There will be personnel specialized in their respective areas and co-ordination among the diverse areas calls for team work.

(5) Complexity : A project is a complex set of activities relating to diverse areas.

(6) Risk and uncertainty : Risk and uncertainty go hand in hand with project. A risk-free, it only means that the element is not apparently visible on the surface and it will be hidden underneath.

(7) Customer specific nature : A project is always customer specific. It is the customer who decides upon the product to be produced or services to be offered and hence it is the responsibility of any organization to go for projects/services that are suited to customer needs.

(8)Change : Changes occur through out the life span of a project as a natural outcome of many environmental factors. The changes may very from minor changes, which may have very little impact on the project, to major changes which may have a big impact or even may change the very nature of the project.

(9)Optimality : A project is always aimed at optimum utilization of resources for the overall development of the economy.

(10) Sub-contracting : A high level of work in a project is done through contractors. The more the complexity of the project, the more will be the extent of contracting.

(11) Unity in diversity : A project is a complex set of thousands of varieties. The varieties are in terms of technology, equipment and materials, machinery and people, work, culture and others.

PROJECT FAMILY TREE

A project normally originates from a plan, national plan or corporate plan. In normal scheme of things, the family tree for a project would be as given below

Plan = National/Corporate plan with target for growth.

Programme = health programme, educational programme, R&D programme.

Project = Power plant, hospital, housing project etc.

Work Package = Water supply, power supply and distribution package.

Task = Award of water supply contract, construction & foundation.

Activity = Excavation, laying of cable, preparation of drawing.

CLASSIFICATION OF PROJECTS

The location, type, technology, size, scope and speed are normally the factors which determine the effort needed in executing a project. Project can be classified under different heads, some of which are shown in figure below:

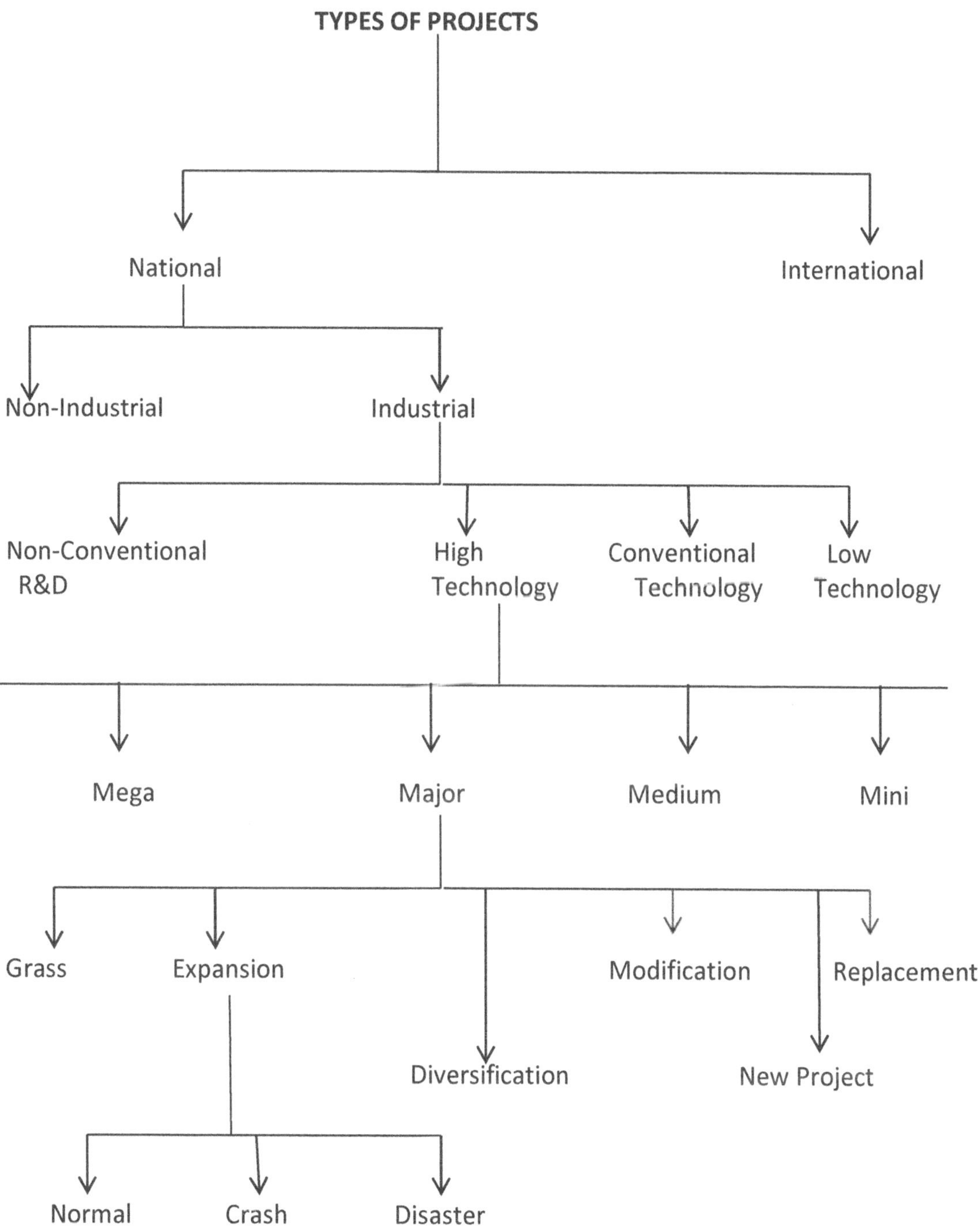

PROJECT SELECTION PROCESS

Identification of a new project is a complex problem. Project selection process starts with the generation of project ideas. In order to select the most promising project, the entrepreneur needs to generate a few ideas about the possible project one can undertake. The project ideas as a process of identification of a project begins with an analytical survey of the economy (also known as pre-investment surveys). The surveys and studies will give us ideas. The process of project selection consists of following stages :

- ➢ Idea generation
- ➢ Environment appraisal.
- ➢ Corporate appraisal
- ➢ Scouting for project ideas.
- ➢ Preliminary screening.
- ➢ Project rating index
- ➢ Sources of positive Net Present Value.
- ➢ Entrepreneur qualities.

Idea Generation :- Project selection process starts with the generation of a project idea. Ideas are based on technological breakthroughs and most of the project ideas are variants of present products or services. To stimulate the flow of ideas, the following are helpful:

SWOT Analysis :- SWOT is an acronym for strengths, weaknesses, opportunities and threats. SWOT analysis represents conscious, deliberate and systematic effort by an organisation to identify opportunities that can be profitably exploited by it. Periodic SWOT analysis facilitates the generation of ideas. Operational objectives of a firm may be one or more of the following.

- Cost reduction.
- Productivity improvement.
- Increase in capacity utilisation.
- Improvement in contribution margin.

Fostering a conducive climate :- To tap the creativity of people and to harness their entrepreneurial skills, a conducive organisation climate has to be fostered. Two conspicuous examples of organisation which have been exceptionally successful in tapping the creativity of employees are the Bell Telephone Laboratory and the 3M Corporation. While the former has succeeded in harnessing creativity by providing an unconstrained environment, the latter has effectively nurtured the entrepreneurial skills of its employees as sources of idea generation. The project ideas can be generated from various internal and external sources. These are :-

- Knowledge of market, products, and services.
- Knowledge of potential customer choice.
- Emerging trends in demand for particular product.
- Scope for producing substitute product.
- Market survey & research.
- Going through Professional magazines.
- Making visits to trade and exhibitions.
- Government guidelines & policy.
- Ideas given by the experienced person.
- Ideas by own experience.
- SWOT analysis.

Environment appraisal :- An entrepreneur or a firm systematically appraise the environment and assess its competitive abilities. For the purposes of monitoring, the business environment may be divided into six broad sectors as shown in fig. below The key elements of the environment are as follow :

Economic Sector

• State of the economy
• Overall rate of growth
• Cyclical fluctuations
• Inflation rate
• Growth rate of primary, secondary and territory sector
• Growth rate of world economy
• Trade surplus and deficits
• Balance of Payment

Government Sector

• Industrial policy
• Government programmes and projects
• Tax structure
• EXIM policy
• Financing norms
• Subsidies incentives and concessions
• Monetary policy

Technological Sector

• Emergence of new technologies
• Access to technical know-how, foreign as well as indigenous

Socio-demographic Sector

• Population trends
• Age shifts in population
• Income distribution
• Educational profile
• Employment of women
• Attitudes toward consumption and investment

Competition Sector

• Number of firms in the industry and the market share of the top few
• Degree of homogeneity and differentiation among the products
• Entry barrier
• Comparison with substitutes in term of quality and price
• Marketing polices and practices

Supplier Sector

• Availability and cost of raw material
• Availability and cost of energy
• Availability and cost of capital

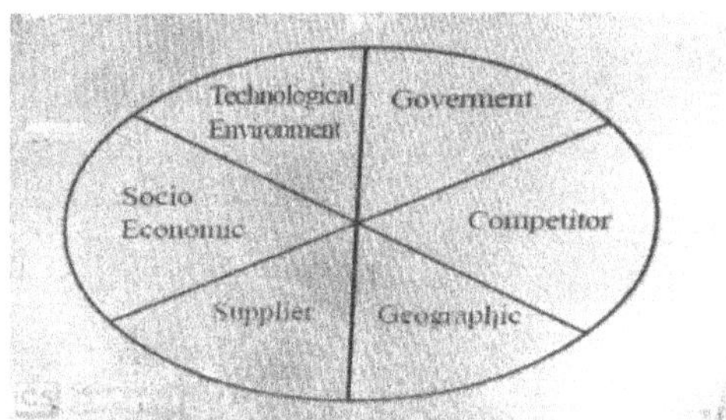

Business Environment

Corporate Appraisal :- A realistic appraisal of corporate strengths and weaknesses is essential for identifying investment opportunities which can be profitably exploited. The broad areas of corporate appraisal and the important aspects to be considered under them are as follow :

Marketing and Distribution

- Market Image
- Product Line
- Product Mix
- Distribution Channels
- Customer loyalty
- Marketing & distribution costs

Production and Operations

- Condition and capacity of plant and machinery
- Availability of raw material and power
- Degree of vertical integration
- Locational advantage
- Cost structure

Research and Development

- Research capabilities of the firm
- Track record of new product developments
- Laboratories and testing facilities
- Coordination between research and operations

Corporate Resources and Personnel

- Corporate image
- Dynamism of top management
- Relation with government and regulatory agencies
- State of industry relations

Finance and Accounting

- **Financial leverage and borrowing capacity**
- Cost of capital
- Tax structure
- Relation with share holders and creditors
- Accounting & control system
- Cash flow and liquidity

PROJECT LIFE CYCLE

A project is not a one shot activity. Even a shooting star has a time and life span. Project lifecycle is spread over a period of time. There is an unavoidable gestation period for the complex of activities involved to attain the objectives in view. This gestation period, however, varies from project to project but it is possible to describe, in general term, the time phasing of project planning activities common to most projects. The principal stages in the life of a project are :

- Identification
- Initial formulation
- Evaluation (selection or rejection)
- Final formulation (or selection)
- Implementation
- Completion and operation

Development projects are expressly designed to solve the varied problems of the economics whether in the short or long run. The surveys or in depth studies would locate the problems and the project planner will have to identify the projects that would solve the problems most effectively. At this stage, we are concerned with the kind of action and type of project that would be required in rather broad term. In other words the surveys and studies will give us ideas and throw up suggestions which would be worked out in detail later and then evaluated objectively before being accepted for implementation.What types of surveys and studies are to be undertaken? The current sociopoliticaleconomic situation has to be critically assessed. It will also be necessary to review it in its historical perspective necessitating the undertaking of a survey of the behaviour and growth of the economy during the preceding decades. On the basis of past trends, extrapolation may be made of future possible trends and tendencies, short and long term. There are scientific techniques for doing so which can be broadly grouped as forecasting methodology. It is however not sufficient to view the socio-economic panorama on the historical canvas. More detailed investigations from an operational point of view would be called for in respect of each economic sector.

Initial Formulation :- Identification is only the beginning in the lifecycle of a project.Having identified the prospective projects, the details of each project will have to be worked out and analysed in order to determine which of them could be reckoned as suitable for inclusion in the plan, allocate funds and put into execution. As a follow up to the finding of techno-economic surveys, and number of feasibility study group are set up, as the name implies to examine the possibility of formulating suitable projects and to put concrete proposals in sufficient detail to enable authorities concerned to consider the feasibility of the proposal submitted.

Evaluation or Project Appraisal :- After the socio-economic problems of an economy have been determined and developments objectives and strategies agreed, concrete steps have to be taken. The main form this takes is that of formulating appropriate development projects to achieve plan objectives and meet the development needs of the economy. Proposals relating to them are then put to the plan authorities for consideration and inclusion in the plan. These proposals as pointed out above take the following forms of feasibility studies :

- Commercial viability
- Economic feasibility
- Financial feasibility

• Technical feasibility
• Management

The scope for scrutiny under each of these five heads would necessarily render their careful assessment and the examination of all possible alternative approaches. The process almost invariably involves making decision relating to technology, scale,location,costs and benefits, time of completion (gestation period), degree of risk and uncertainty, financial viability, organisation and management, availability of inputs,know-how, labour etc. The detailed analysis is set down in what is called a **feasibility report.**

Feasibilty study: The feasibility dtudy ic concerned with first four phases of capital budgeting viz planning, analysis, selection(evaluation),and financing and involves market,technical,financial,economic and ecologic analysis as shown in the exhibit

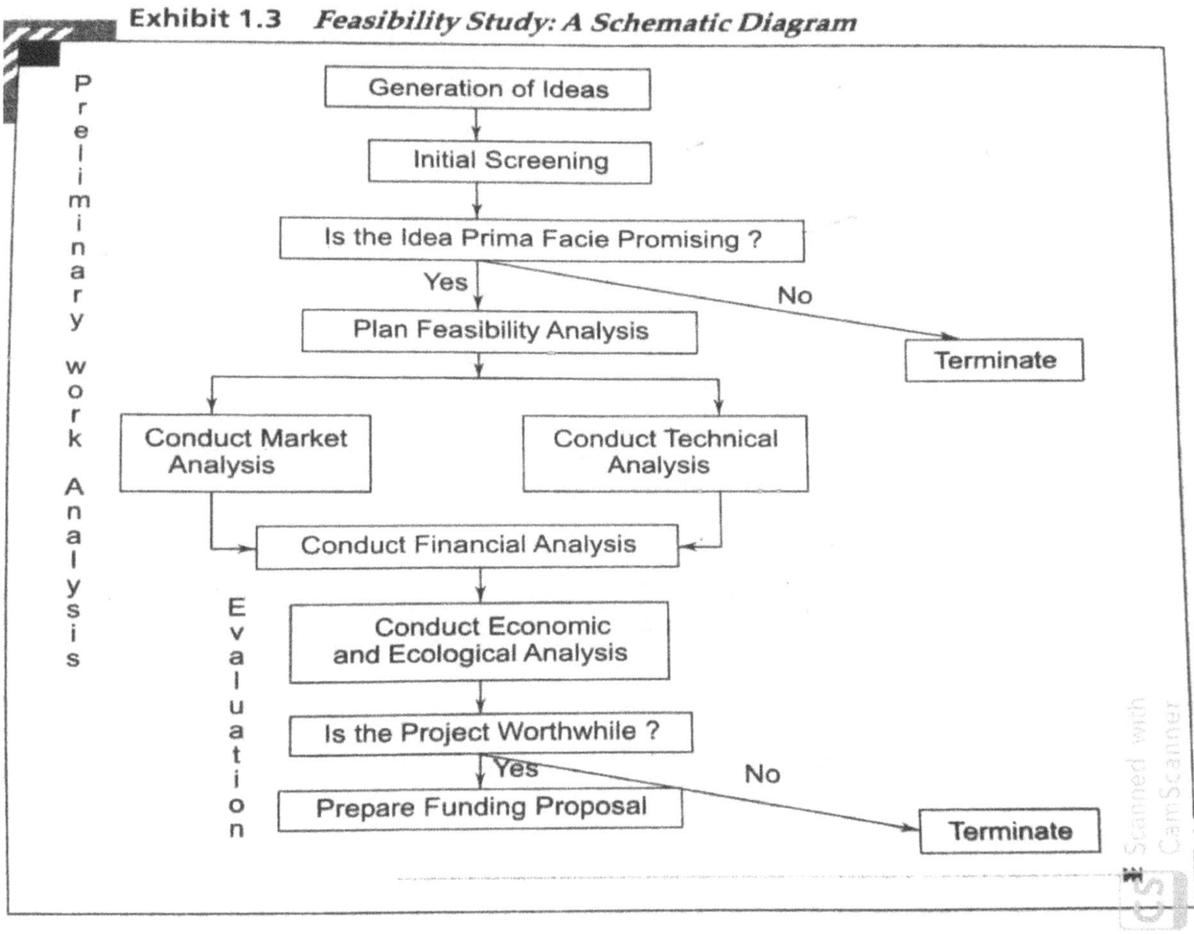

Exhibit 1.3   *Feasibility Study: A Schematic Diagram*

Formulation :- Once a project has been appraised and approved, next step would logically, appear to that of implementation. This is, however, not necessarily true, if the approval is conditional to certain modifications being affected or for other reasons,such as availability of funds, etc. The implementation stage will be reached only after these pre-conditions have been fulfilled. Project formulation divides the process of project development into eight distinct and sequential stages. These stages are

- General information
- Project description
- Market potential
- Capital costs and sources of finance
- Assessment of working capital requirement
- Other financial aspect
- Economic and social variables.

Project Implementation :- Last but not the least, every entrepreneur should draw an implementation time table for his project. The network having been prepared, the project authorities are now ready to embark on the main task of implementation the project. To begin with successful implementation will depend on how well the network has been designed. However, during the course of implementation, many factors arise which cannot be anticipated or adequately taken note of in advance and built into the initial network. A number of network techniques have been developed for project implementation. Some of them are PERT, CPM, Graphical Evaluation and Review Technique (GERT), Workshop Analysis Scheduling Programme (WRSP) and Line of Balance (LOB).

Project Completion :- It is often debated as to the point at which the project life cycle is completed. The cycle is completed only when the development objectives are realized.

PROJECT REPORT

In simple words project report or business plan is a written statement of what an entrepreneur proposes to take up. It is a kind of course of action what the entrepreneur hopes to achieve in his business and how he is going to achieve it. In other words, project report serves like a road map to reach the destination determined by the entrepreneur.

Contents of Project Report

- General Information
- Promoter
- Location
- Land and Building
- Plant and Machinery
- Production process
- Utilities
- Transport and communication
- Raw material
- Manpower
- Product
- Market

PROJECT APPRAISAL

Project appraisal means the assessment of a project. Project appraisal is made for both proposed and executed projects. In case of former project appraisal is called ex-ante analysis and in case of letter 'post-ante analysis'. Here, project appraisal is related to a proposed project.

Project appraisal is a cost and benefits analysis of different aspects of proposed project with an objective to adjudge its viability. A project involves employment of scarce resources. An entrepreneur needs to appraise various alternative projects before allocating the scarce resources for the best project. Thus project appraisal helps select the best project among available alternative projects. For appraising a projects its economic, financial, technical market, managerial and social aspect are analysed. Financial institutions carry out project appraisal to assess its creditworthiness before extending finance to a project.

Method of Project Appraisal/ Principles of Project Analysis

Appraisal of a proposed project includes the following analysis :

1 Economic analysis

2 Financial analysis

3 Market analysis

4 Technical analysis

5 Managerial competence

6 Ecological analysis

Economic Analysis :

Under economic analysis the aspects highlighted include

- Requirements for raw material
- Level of capacity utilization
- Anticipated sales
- Anticipated expenses
- Proposed profits
- Estimated demand

It is said that a business should have always a volume of profit clearly in view which will govern other economic variable like sales, purchase, expenses and alike.

Financial Analysis

Finance is one of the most important prerequisites to establish an enterprise. It nis finance only that facilitates an entrepreneur to bring together the labour, machines and raw materials to combine them to produce goods. In order to adjudge the financial viability of the project, the following aspects need to be carefully analysed :

- Cost of capital
- Means of finance
- Estimates of sales and production
- Cost of production
- Working capital requirement and its financing
- Estimates of working results
- Break-even point
- Projected cash flow
- Projected balance sheet.

The activity level of an enterprise expressed as capacity utilization needs to be well spelled out. However the enterprise sometimes fails to achieve the targeted level of capacity due to various business vicissitudes like unforeseen shortage of raw material, unexpected disruption in powersupply, instability to penetrate the market mechanism etc.

Market Analysis

Before the production actually starts, the entrepreneur needs to anticipate the possible market for the product. He has to anticipate who will be the possible customer for his product and where his product will be sold. This is because production has no value for the producer unless it is sold. In fact, the potential of the market constitutes the determinant of possible reward from entrepreneurial career.Thus knowing the anticipated market for the product to be produced become an important element in business plan. The commonly used methods to estimate the demand for a product are as follows. :

1 Opinion polling method

In this method, the opinion of the ultimate users. This may be attempted with the help of either a complete survey of all customers or by selecting a few consuming units out of the relevant population.

2. Life Cycle Segmentation Analysis

It is well established that like a man, every product has its own life span. In practice, a product sells slowly in the beginning. Barked by sales promotion strategies over period its sales pick up. In the due course of time the peak sale is reached. After nthat point the sales begins to decline. After sometime, the product loses its demand and dies. This is natural death of a product. Thus, every product passes through its life cycle. The product life cycle has been divided into the following five stage : Introduction, Growth, Maturity, Saturation and Decline. The sales of the product varies from stage to stage as shown in figure No. 1.4

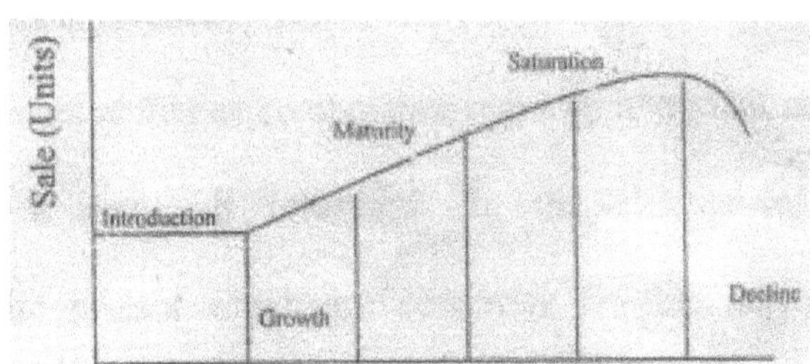

Time Period
Product Life Cycle

Considering the above five stages of a product life cycle, the sale at different stages can be anticipated.

Technical Analysis

Technical analysis implies the adequacy of the proposed plant and equipment to prescribed norms. It should be ensured whether the required know how is available with the entrepreneur. The following inputs concerned in the project should also be taken into consideration.

> Availability of Land and site
> Availability of Water Power, transport, communication facilities.
> Availability of servicing facilities like machine shop, electric repair shop etc.
> Coping with anti pollution law
> Availability of work force
> Availability of required raw material as per quantity and quality.

Management Competence

Management ability or competence plays an important role in making an enterprise a success. In the absence of Managerial Competence the project which are otherwise feasible may fail. On the contrary, even a poor project may become a successful one with good managerial ability. Hence, while doing project appraisal, the managerial competence or talent of the promoter should be taken into consideration.

Ecological Analysis

In recent years, environmental concerns have assumed great deal of significance.Ecological analysis should also be done particularly for major projects which have significant implication like power plant and irrigation schemes, and environmental pollution industries like bulk-drugs, chemical and leather processing. The key factors considered for ecological analysis are :

> Environmental damage
> Restoration measure

TOOLS AND TECHNIQUES FOR PROJECT MANAGEMENT

There are several tools and techniques which would contribute significantly towards effective project management these can be broadly grouped under the following heads :

1. Project selection techniques
   (a) Cost benefit analysis and
   (b) Risk and sensitivity analysis

2. Project execution planning techniques
   (a) Work breakdown structure (WBS)
   (b) project execution plan (PEP)
   (c) Project responsibility matrix and
   (d) Project management manual

3. Project scheduling and coordinating techniques
   (a) Bar charts
   (b) Life cycle curves
   (c) Line of balance (LOB) and
   (d) Networking techniques (PERT/CPM)

4. Project monitoring and progressing techniques
   (a) Progress measurement technique (PROMPT)
   (b) Performance monitoring technique (PERMIT) and
   (c) Updating, reviewing and reporting technique (URT)

5. Project cost and productivity control techniques
   (a) Productivity budgeting techniques
   (b) Value engineering (VE) and
   (c) COST/WBS

6. Project communication and clean-up techniques
   (a) Control room and
   (b) Computerised information systems

THE PROJECT MANAGER'S ROLES & RESPONSIBILITIES

As things stand today, non of the present generation project manager, including the very successful ones, come from any of our management schools. They were just given the job-some succeeded and others did not. Those who succeeded are not many, because only a handful of projects in India were ever completed on time, within budget and performed to expectations. While the failures of these projects had been analysed in many seminars and workshops, the role of project managers and their development did not form the subject of any serious discussion. There could be two reasons for this: (a) Perhaps no one thinks that success or failure of a project depends on the project manager; and (b) It may also be that no one considers them as a special breed of managers. Surprisingly, even some of the practising project managers themselves subscribe to these views. The basic roles and responsibilities of a project manager that we are referring to could be grouped under twelve heads :

1 Defining and maintaining the integrity of a project;
2 Development of project execution plan;
3 Organization for execution of the plan;
4 Setting of targets and development of systems and procedures for accomplishment of project objectives and targets;
5 Negotiation for commitments;
6 Direction, coordination and control of project activities;
7 Contract management;
8 Non-human resource management including fiscal matters;
9 Problem-solving;
10 Man management;
11 Satisfaction of customer, Government and the public; and
12 Achievement of project objectives, cash surplus and higher productivity.

TOOLS FOR IDENTIFYING INVESTMENT OPPORTUNITIES

An organization has many occasions when it has to invest for achieving its goals.The finance department of the organization remains busy in finding the opportunities for investing in order to coup the fluctuations and trends in th ,aqrkets and also for the survival of organization Among the opportunities of investments following are discussed as under:

- Replacement and modernization
- Capacity expansion
- Vertical integration
- Concentric diversification
- Conglomerate diversification
- Divestment

Replacement and Modernisation

It means to maintain the production capacity of the firm, improve quality, and reduce costs. Without such investments, which are undertaken more or less routinely by well managed firms, the competitive strength of the firm in its existing line of business can be significantly impaired.

Capacity Expansion

When a company anticipates growth in the market size of its product range or increase in the market share enjoyed by it in its product range, expansion of the capacity of the product range would have great appeal. Such an expansion offers several advantages : familiarity with technology, production methods and market conditions, lower capital costs due to the existence of surplus capacity in certain sections of the factory, reduction in unit overhead costs because of larger volume or production.

Vertical Integration

Vertical integration may be of two types : backward integration and forward integration. Backward integration involves manufacture of raw materials and components required for the existing operations of the company. For example, Reliance Industries Limited set up a unit for the manufacture of polyester filament yarn required for its textile units. Forward integration involves the manufacture of products which use the existing products of the company as input. For example, Bharat Forge Company set up a automotive axles unit which uses its forgings as input.

Concentric Diversification

Many companies seek to widen their product range by adding related products. For example, a soap manufacturer may enter the field of detergents; a scooter producer may add motorcycles to its product line; a truck manufacturer may go for passenger cars.

Conglomerate Diversification

Conglomerate diversification involves investment in fields unrelated to the existing line of business. For example, when an engineering company like Larsen and Toubro invests in shipping it is a case of conglomerate diversification.

Divestment

Divestment is the opposite of investment. It involves termination or liquidation of the plant or even a division of a firm. The disposal of the Chembur plant of Union Carbide to Oswal Agro is an example of divestment.

PORTFOLIO PLANNING TOOLS

To guide the process of strategic planning and resource allocation, several portfolio planning tools have been developed. Two such tools highly relevant in this
context are :
BCG Product Portfolio Matrix
General Electric's Stoplight Matrix

BCG Product Matrix

A tool for strategic (product) planning and resource allocation, the BostonConsulting Group (BCG) product portfolio matrix analyses products on the basis of(a) relative market share and (b) industry growth rate. The BCG matrix, shown in Exhibit blow classifies products into four broad categories as follows

BCG Product Portfolio Matrix

BCG Product Portfolio Matrix

Relative Market Share

		High	Low
Industry Growth Rate	High	Stars	Question marks
	Low	Cash cows	Dogs

- **Stars** Product which enjoy a high, market share and a high growth rate are referred to as stars.
- **Question marks** Products with high growth potential but low present market share are called question marks.
- **Cash Cows** Products which enjoy a relatively high market share but low growth potential are called cash cows.
- **Dogs** Products with low markets share and limited growth potential are referred to as dogs.

From the above description, it is broadly clear that cash cows generate funds and dogs, if divested, release funds. On the other hand, stars and question marks require further commitment of funds.

General Electric's Stoplight Matrix

The General Electric Company of US is widely respected for the sophistication maturity, and quality of its planning systems. The matrix developed by his company for guiding resource allocation is called the General Electric's Stoplight Matrix. It calls for analyzing various products of the firm in terms of two key issues.

- **Business Strength** How strong is the firm vis-a-vis its competitors ?
- **Industry attractiveness :-** What is the attractiveness or potential of the industry.

Industry Attractiveness		Business Strength		
		Strong	Average	Weak
	High	Invest	Invest	Invest
	Medium	Invest	Hold	Divest
	Low	Hold	Divest	Divest

General Electric's Stoplight Matrix

Strategic Position and Action Evaluation (Space)

SPACE is an approach to hammer out an appropriate strategic posture for a firm arid its individual business. An extension of the two-dimensional portfolio analysis, SPACE involves a consideration of four dimensions :

- Company's competitive advantage.
- Company's financial strength.
- Industry strength.
- Environmental stability

PUBLIC SECTOR PROJECT

The term 'public project' is an ambiguous one, but in very broad terms, it refers to a project that is financed by a government and is typically owned, and may be operated by the government. This can include major infrastructure works such as roads, bridges, dams, railways, tunnels, and so on, or public facilities such as hospitals, schools, prisons, libraries, leisure centers, and so on. As public projects are generally funded by tax revenue, they are typically subject to a greater level of scrutiny, and greater transparency is required in the bidding and award procedures. Public projects often publish their requirements and request bids openly, with received bids considered in an open and transparent way. The government can also stipulate certain criteria that a supplier must fulfill in order to be awarded a public contract, such as; minimum wage levels, reporting procedures, and so on. The public sector (also called the state sector) is the part of the economy composed of both public services and public enterprises.Public sectors include public goods and governmental services such as the military, law enforcement, infrastructure (public roads, bridges, tunnels, water supply, sewers, electrical grids, telecommunications, etc.), public transit, public education, along with care and those working for the government itself, such as elected officials. The public sector might provide services that a non-payer cannot be excluded from (such as street lighting), services which benefit all of society rather than just the individual who uses the service. Public enterprises, or state-owned enterprises, are self-financing commercial enterprises that are under public ownership which provide various private goods and services for sale and usually operate on a commercial basis.

PRIVATE SECTOR PROJECTS

The private sector project are the part of the economy that is run by individuals and companies for profit and is not state controlled. Therefore, it encompasses all for-profit businesses that are not owned or operated by the government. Companies and corporations that are government run are part of what is known as the public sector, while charities and other nonprofit organizations are part of the voluntary sector. The private sector consists of all privately owner, for-profit businesses in the economy. The private sector tends to make up a larger share of the economy in free market, capitalist based societies.Private sector businesses can also collaborate with government run agencies in arrangements called public-private partnershipsThe private sector is the segment of a national economy that is owned, controlled, and managed by private individuals or enterprises. The private sector has a goal of making money and employs more workers than the public sector. A private sector organization is created by forming a new enterprise or privatizing a public sector organization. A large private sector corporation may be privately or publicly traded. Businesses in the private sector drive down prices for goods and services while competing for consumers' money; in theory, customers do not want to pay more for something when they can buy the same item elsewhere at a lower cost.The entities that form the private sector include:

- Sole proprietorships
- Partnerships
- Small and mid-sized businesses
- Large corporations and multinationals
- Professional and trade associations
- Trade unions

Private and Public Sector Differences

The private sector employs workers through individual business owners, corporations or other non-government agencies. Jobs include those in manufacturing, financial services, professions, hospitality, or other non-government positions. Workers are paid with part of the company's profits. Private sector workers tend to have more pay increases, more career choices, greater opportunities for promotions, less job security, and less comprehensive benefit plans than public sector workers. Working in a more competitive marketplace often means longer hours in a more demanding environment than working for the government.

The public sector employs workers through the federal, state or local government. Typical civil service jobs are in healthcare, teaching, emergency services, armed forces, and various regulatory and administrative agencies. Workers are paid through a portion of the government's tax dollars. Public sector workers tend to have more comprehensive benefit plans and more job security than private sector workers; once a probationary period concludes, many government positions become permanent appointments. Moving among public sector positions while retaining the same benefits, holiday entitlements, and sick pay is relatively easy while receiving pay increases and promotions is difficult. Working with a public agency provides a more stable work environment free of market pressures, unlike working in the private sector.

SOCIAL AND COMMERCIAL PROFITABILITY ANALYSIS

    Social or National Profitability

Public projects like road, railway, bridge and other transport projects, irrigation, projects, power projects, etc for which socioeconomic considerations play a significant part, rather than mere commercial profitability. Such projects are analysis for their net socioeconomic benefits and the profitability analysis of such projects is known as social or national profitability analysis which is nothing but the socioeconomic cost benefit analysis done at the national level.

Steps involved in determination of social or national profitability:-

National/Social profitability analysis takes into account the real cost of direct costs and real benefit of direct benefits,. For instance, some of the inputs may be subsidized. Only the subsidized prices of input is what is relevant for assessing commercial profitability. However the national profitability analysis takes into account the real cost of inputs i.e. cost of input had they not been subsidized. Accordingly the required adjustment to direct cost of input are made for national profitability analysis.

National/Social profitability analysis takes into account the indirect costs and indirect benefits to the nation.While a nation bears the indirect, the people of the nation enjoy the indirect benefit. Hence indirect costs and benefits are given due recognition and accounted for in social cost benefit analysis. It is however difficult to assess exactly the quantum of indirect costs and indirect benefits.Â Suppose construction of a bridge over a river. It's indirect benefits may include improved communication facilities reduction in transportation costs, reduction in traveling time etc. while the indirect cost may include acquisition of private land by the state, removal of industrial, commercial, agricultural activities that prevailed in the land that was acquired disturbance of ecological balance etc.

National/Social profitability analysis can thus be regarded as a refinement over commercial appraisal taking the hidden factors into account. National/Social profitability analysis is mainly used for evaluating public investment projects. From the society's standpoint, the project should maximize the aggregate consumption or the addition to the flow of goods or services in the economy investor looks for maximization on his individual basis, the society's interest should look for maximization of the total output of the economy. The need total thus arises to have an analysis done of social costs and social benefits. The various inputs required for the project are drawls out of the resources of the economy and constitutes social costs. And the output of the any of the public project represent social benefits. The input of goods and services and the outputs should be valued with reference to their relative value to society.

    Commercial or Financial profitability

The national development point of view there are always more projects than there are resources and hence the necessity to appraise projects for selection. While the obvious choice will be the projects with higher returns the complexity arises because of the need to appraise projected outcome based on forecasts in a world of uncertainly, particularly in the context of endemic inflation. In the case of large projects, particularly public sector projects involving the building up of infrastructure it is essential to assess the social merits of the investment proposals.

Projects emanate from diverse and dispersed sources, such as individuals firms or institutions, and government at the state and central levels. In instance where the state government is not the owner of the business. The traditional yard stick of commercial or financial profitability is used for selection of projects for implementation. The financial benefits get related to the financial costs of the project and if there is a net surplus the project merit choice.While the process of selection of individual projects thus meets the profit criteria of the individual investors or promoters, the combination of choices may not necessarily result in the most socials profitable allocation of resources. For developing economies this is the very important factor but it cannot be ignored.

Commercial or financial profitability as the sole deciding factor has two major limitations viz.

Financial or market values seldom match with social values and

What is beneficial to one segment of society may not necessary be so to the entire society.

In financial analysis the market values of input and outputs are reckoned and compared. And since market distortions are many these values fail to reflect the relative worth on the society's value scale. From society's stand point, goods and services should be valued in terms of relative contributions to consumption. In the same manner the social value of resource should be reckoned interns of its opportunity cost, represented by the output or consumption value that it is capable of yielding in its next best alternative use.

In a free market economy the dominance of the forces of demand and supply has the effect of the market prices being kept close to social valuation. In a developing economy however there are several distortions entering into the market prices and they are far removed from their social valuation. The distortions arise from the monopolistic status of many large enterprise a system of administered prices in a controlled economy and from various government policy measures such as taxes, duties, controls and foreign exchange regulations.

A project may confer considerable good to society that does not get reflected in financial projections others though financially very rewarding may have some harmful effects on society that the financial results fail to interpret. These effects that are outside the purview of financial projections are known as externalities and are essential ingredients in the social profitability computations. The emphasis in social cost benefit analysis is the import on the whole society and not one segment.

Concept of Entrepreneurship:

The word "entrepreneur" is derived from the French verb enterprendre, which means 'to undertake'. This refers to those who "undertake" the risk of new enterprises. An enterprise is created by an entrepreneur. The process of creation is called "entrepreneurship".

Entrepreneurship is a process of actions of an entrepreneur who is a person always in search of something new and exploits such ideas into gainful opportunities by accepting the risk and uncertainty with the enterprise.

Characteristics of Entrepreneurship: Entrepreneurship is characterized by the following features:

1. *Economic and dynamic activity:* Entrepreneurship is an economic activity because it involves the creation and operation of an enterprise with a view to creating value or wealth by ensuring optimum utilisation of scarce resources. Since this value creation

activity is performed continuously in the midst of uncertain business environment, therefore, entrepreneurship is regarded as a dynamic force.

2. _Related to innovation_: Entrepreneurship involves a continuous search for new ideas. Entrepreneurship compels an individual to continuously evaluate the existing modes of business operations so that more efficient and effective systems can be evolved and adopted. In other words, entrepreneurship is a continuous effort for synergy (optimization of performance) in organizations.

3. _Profit potential_: "Profit potential is the likely level of return or compensation to the entrepreneur for taking on the risk of developing an idea into an actual business venture." Without profit potential, the efforts of entrepreneurs would remain only an abstract and a theoretical leisure activity.

4. _Risk bearing_: The essence of entrepreneurship is the 'willingness to assume risk' arising out of the creation and implementation of new ideas. New ideas are always tentative and their results may not be instantaneous and positive. An entrepreneur has to have patience to see his efforts bear fruit. In the intervening period (time gap between the conception and implementation of an idea and its results), an entrepreneur has to assume risk. If an entrepreneur does not have the willingness to assume risk, entrepreneurship would never succeed.

Entrepreneurial Process: Entrepreneurship is a process, a journey, not the destination; a means, not an end. All the successful entrepreneurs like Bill Gates (Microsoft), Warren Buffet (Hathaway), Gordon Moore (Intel) Steve Jobs (Apple Computers), Jack Welch (GE) GD Birla, Jamshedji Tata and others all went through this process. To establish and run an enterprise it is divided into three parts – the entrepreneurial job, the promotion, and the operation. Entrepreneurial job is restricted to two steps, i.e., generation of an idea and preparation of feasibility report. In this article, we shall restrict ourselves to only these two aspects of entrepreneurial process.

The Entrepreneurial Process

1. **Idea Generation**: To generate an idea, the entrepreneurial process has to pass through three stages:
    a. Germination: This is like seeding process, not like planting seed. It is more like the natural seeding. Most creative ideas can be linked to an individual's interest or curiosity about a specific problem or area of study.
    b. Preparation: Once the seed of interest curiosity has taken the shape of a focused idea, creative people start a search for answers to the problems. Inventors will go on for setting up laboratories; designers will think of engineering new product ideas and marketers will study consumer buying habits.
    c. Incubation: This is a stage where the entrepreneurial process enters the sub•conscious intellectualization. The sub-conscious mind joins the unrelated ideas so as to find a resolution.
2. **Feasibility study**: Feasibility study is done to see if the idea can be commercially viable. It

passes through two steps:

a. Illumination: After the generation of idea, this is the stage when the idea is thought of as a realistic creation. The stage of idea blossoming is critical because ideas by themselves have no meaning.

b. Verification: This is the last thing to verify the idea as realistic and useful for application. Verification is concerned about practicality to implement an idea and explore its usefulness to the society and the entrepreneur.

Importance of Entrepreneurship:

Entrepreneurship offers the following benefits:

1. _Development of managerial capabilities:_ The biggest significance of entrepreneurship lies in the fact that it helps in identifying and developing managerial capabilities of entrepreneurs. An entrepreneur studies a problem, identifies its alternatives, compares the alternatives in terms of cost and benefits implications, and finally chooses the best alternative.This exercise helps in sharpening the decision making skills of an entrepreneur. Besides, these managerial capabilities are used by entrepreneurs in creating new technologies and products in place of older technologies and products resulting in higher performance.

2. _Creation of organisations_: Entrepreneurship results into creation of organisations when entrepreneurs assemble and coordinate physical, human and financial resources and direct them towards achievement of objectives through managerial skills.

3. _Improving standards of living:_By creating productive organisations, entrepreneurship helps in making a wide variety of goods and services available to the society which results into higher standards of living for the people.Possession of luxury cars, computers, mobile phones, rapid growth of shopping malls, etc. are pointers to the rising living standards of people, and all this is due to the efforts of entrepreneurs.

4. _Means of economic development_: Entrepreneurship involves creation and use of innovative ideas, maximisation of output from given resources, development of managerial skills, etc., and all these factors are so essential for the economic development of a country.

Entrepreneurship is a complex phenomenon influenced by the interplay of a wide variety of factors.Some of the important factors are listed below:

1. Personality Factors:

Personal factors, becoming core competencies of entrepreneurs, include:

(a) Initiative (does things before being asked for)

(b) Proactive (identification and utilization of opportunities)

(c) Perseverance (working against all odds to overcome obstacles and never complacent with success)

(d) Problem-solver (conceives new ideas and achieves innovative solutions)

(e) Persuasion (to customers and financiers for patronisation of his business and develops & maintains relationships)

(f) Self-confidence (takes and sticks to his decisions)

(g) Self-critical (learning from his mistakes and experiences of others)

(h) A Planner (collects information, prepares a plan, and monitors performance)

(i) Risk-taker (the basic quality).

2. Environmental factors: These factors relate to the conditions in which an entrepreneur has to work. Environmental factors such as political climate, legal system, economic and social conditions, market situations, etc. contribute significantly towards the growth of entrepreneurship. For example, political stability in a country is absolutely essential for smooth economic activity.

Frequent political protests, bandhs, strikes, etc. hinder economic activity and entrepreneurship. Unfair trade practices, irrational monetary and fiscal policies, etc. are a roadblock to the growth of entrepreneurship. Higher income levels of people, desire for new products and sophisticated technology, need for faster means of transport and communication, etc. are the factors that stimulate entrepreneurship.Thus, it is a combination of both personal and environmental factors that influence entrepreneurship and brings in desired results for the individual, the organisation and the society.

2. Imitating entrepreneurs:

These entrepreneurs are people who follow the path shown by innovative entrepreneurs. They imitate innovative entrepreneurs because the environment in which they operate is such that it does not permit them to have creative and innovative ideas on their own.Such entrepreneurs are found in countries and situations marked with weak industrial and institutional base which creates difficulties in initiating innovative ideas.In our country also, a large number of such entrepreneurs are found in every field of business activity and they fulfill their need for achievement by imitating the ideas introduced by innovative entrepreneurs.Development of small shopping complexes is the work of imitating entrepreneurs. All the small car manufacturers now are the imitating entrepreneurs.

3. Fabian entrepreneurs:

The dictionary meaning of the term 'fabian' is 'a person seeking victory by delay rather than by a decisive battle'. Fabian entrepreneurs are those individuals who do not show initiative in visualising and implementing new ideas and innovations wait for some development which would motivate them to initiate unless there is an imminent threat to their very existence.

4. Drone entrepreneurs: The dictionary meaning of the term 'drone' is 'a person who lives on the labor of others'. Drone entrepreneurs are those individuals who are satisfied with the existing mode and speed of business activity and show no inclination in gaining market leadership. In other words, drone entrepreneurs are die-hard conservatives and even ready to suffer the loss of business.

5. Social Entrepreneur: Social entrepreneurs drive social innovation and transformation in various fields including education, health, human rights, workers' rights, environment and enterprise development.They undertake poverty alleviation objectives with the zeal of an entrepreneur, business practices and dare to overcome traditional practices and to innovate. Dr Mohammed Yunus of Bangladesh who started Gramin Bank is a case of social entrepreneur.

Functions of an Entrepreneur:

The important functions performed by an entrepreneur are listed below:

1. *Innovation:* An entrepreneur is basically an innovator who tries to develop new technology, products, markets, etc. Innovation may involve doing new things or doing existing things differently. An entrepreneur uses his creative faculties to do new things and exploit opportunities in the market. He does not believe in status quo and is always in search of change.

2. _Assumption of Risk_: An entrepreneur, by definition, is risk taker and not risk shirker. He is always prepared for assuming losses that may arise on account of new ideas and projects undertaken by him. This willingness to take risks allows an entrepreneur to take initiatives in doing new things and marching ahead in his efforts.

3. _Research:_An entrepreneur is a practical dreamer and does a lot of ground-work before taking a leap in his ventures. In other words, an entrepreneur finalizes an idea only after considering a variety of options, analyzing their strengths and weaknesses by applying analytical techniques, testing their applicability, supplementing them with empirical findings, and then choosing the best alternative. It is then that he applies his ideas in practice. The selection of an idea, thus, involves the application of research methodology by an entrepreneur.

4. _Development of Management Skills:_The work of an entrepreneur involves the use of managerial skills which he develops while planning, organizing, staffing, directing, controlling and coordinating the activities of business. His managerial skills get further strengthened when he engages himself in establishing equilibrium between his organization and its environment. However, when the size of business grows considerably, an entrepreneur can employ professional managers for the effective management of business operations.

5. _Overcoming Resistance to Change_: New innovations are generally opposed by people because it makes them change their existing behavior patterns. An entrepreneur always first tries new ideas at his level.It is only after the successful implementation of these ideas that an entrepreneur makes these ideas available to others for their benefit. In this manner, an entrepreneur paves the way for the acceptance of his ideas by others. This is a reflection of his will power, enthusiasm and energy which helps him in overcoming the society's resistance to change.

6. _Catalyst of Economic Development_: An entrepreneur plays an important role in accelerating the pace of economic development of a country by discovering new uses of available resources and maximizing their utilization.

UNIT II

MARKET AND DEMAND ANALYSIS
INTRODUCTION
The exercise of project appraisal often begins with an estimation of the size of the market. Before a detailed study of a project is undertaken, it is necessary to know, at least roughly, the size of the market because the viability of the project depends critically on whether the anticipated level of sales exceeds a certain volume. Many a project has been abandoned because preliminary appraisal revealed a market of inadequate size. This chapter is divided into the following five sections dealing with various aspects of market and demand analysis.
1. Information required for market and demand analysis
2. Secondary sources of information
3. Market survey
4. Demand forecasting
5. Uncertainties in demand forecasting

INFORMATION REQUIRED FOR MARKET AND DEMAND ANALYSIS
The principal types of information required for market and demand analysis relate to-

(i) Effective demand in the past and present
To guage the effective demand in the past and present, the starting point typically is apparent consumption which is defined as-

Production + Imports – exports – changes in stock level

In a competitive market, effective demand and apparent consumption are equal. However, in most of the developing countries, where competitive markets do not exist for a variety of products due to exchange restrictions and controls on production and distribution, the figure of apparent consumption may have to be adjusted for market imperfections. Admittedly, this is often a difficult task.

(ii) Breakdown of demand
To get a deeper insight into the nature of demand, the aggregate (total) market demand may be broken down into demand for different segments of the market. Market segments may be defined by (i) nature of product, (ii) consumer group, and (iii) geographical division.

Nature of product— One generic name often subsumes many different products: steel covers sections, rolled products, and various semi finished products; commercial vehicles cover trucks and buses of various capacities etc.

Consumer groups— Consumers of a product may be divided into industrial consumers and domestic consumers. Industrial consumers may be sub-divided industry-wise. Domestic consumers may be further divided into different income groups.

Geographical division— A geographical breakdown of consumers, particularly for products which have a small value-to-weight relationship and products which require regular, efficient after-sales service is helpful.

(iii) Price

Price statistics must be gathered along with statistics pertaining to physical quantities. It may be helpful to distinguish the following types of prices: (i) manufacturer's price quoted as FOB (free on board) price or CIF (cost, insurance, and freight) price, (ii) landed price for imported goods, (iii) average wholesale price, and (iv) average retail price.

(iv) Methods of distribution and sales promotion

The method of distribution may vary with the nature of product. Capital goods, industrial raw materials or intermediates, and consumer products tend to have differing distribution channels. Further, for a given product, distribution methods may vary. Likewise, methods used for sales promotion (advertising, discounts, gift schemes, etc.) may vary from product to product. The methods of distribution and sales promotion employed presently and their rationale must be studied carefully. Such a study may explain certain patterns of consumption and highlight the difficulties that may be encountered in marketing the proposed products.

(v) Consumers

Two categories of information about the consumers may be required: demographic and sociological information, and attitudinal information. Under the first category, information on the following is required: age, sex, income, avocation, residence, religion, customs, beliefs, and social background. Under the second category, information on the following is required-preferences, intentions, attitudes, habits, and responses.

(vi) Governmental policy

The role of government in influencing the demand and market for a product may be significant. Governmental plans, policies, legislations, and fiats which have a bearing on the market and demand of the product under examination should be studied. These are reflected in: production targets in national plans, import and export trade controls, import duties, export incentives, excise duties, sales tax, industrial licensing,preferential purchases, credit controls, financial regulations, and subsidies/penalties of various kinds.

(vii) Supply and competition

It is necessary to know the existing sources of supply and whether they are foreign or domestic. For domestic sources of supply information along the following lines may be gathered: location, present production capacity, planned expansion, capacity utilization level, bottlenecks inproduction, and cost structure.Competition from substitutes and near-substitutes should be examined because almost any good may be replaced by some other good as a result of changes in relative prices, quality, availability, promotional strategies, consumer taste, and other factors.

SECONDARY SOURCES OF INFORMATION

The information required for demand and market analysis is usually obtained partly from secondary sources and partly through a market survey. In marketing research, a distinction is usually made between primary information and secondary information. Primary information refers to information which is collected for the first time to meet the specific purpose on hand; secondary information, in contrast, is information which is in existence and which has been gathered in some other context. Secondary information provides the base and the starting point for market and demand analysis. It indicates what is known and often provides leads and cues for further investigation.

General secondary sources of information

The important sources of secondary information useful for market and demand analysis in India are mentioned below-

Census of India— A decennial publication of the Government of India, it provides information on population, demographic characteristics,household size and composition, and maps.

National sample survey reports— Issued from time to time by the Cabinet Secretariat, Government of India, these reports present information on various economic and social aspects like patterns of consumption,distribution of households by the size of consumer expenditure,distribution of industries, and characteristics of the economically active population. The information presented in these reports is obtained from a nationally representative sample by the interview method.

Plan reports— Issued by the Planning Commission usually at the beginning, middle, and end of the five-year plans, these reports and documents provide a wealth of information on plan proposals, physical and financial targets, actual outlays, accomplishments, etc.

Statistical abstract of the Indian Union— An annual publication of the Central Statistical Organisation, it provides, *inter alia*, demographic information, estimates of national income, and agricultural and industrial statistics.

India Year Book— An annual publication of the Ministry of Information and Broadcasting, it provides wide ranging information on economic and other aspects.

Other publications— Among other publications mention may be made of the following:
 (i) Weekly Bulletin of Industrial Licences, Import Licences and Export Licences (published by the Government of India); (ii) studies of the economic division of the State Trading Corporation; (iii) commodity reports and other studies of the Indian institute of Foreign Trade; (iv) studies and reports of export promotion councils and commodity boards; and (v) Annual report on Currency and Finance (issued by Reserve Bankof India).

Evaluation of secondary information

While secondary information is available economically and readily (provided the market analyst is able to locate it) its reliability, accuracy, and relevance for the purpose under consideration must be carefully examined. The market analyst should seek to know (i) Who gathered the information? What was the objective? (ii) When was information gathered? When was it published? (iii) How representative was the period for which information was gathered? (iv) Have the terms in the study been carefully and unambiguously gathered? (v) What was the target population? (vi) How was the sample chosen? (vii) How representative was the sample? (viii) How satisfactory was the process of information gathering? (ix) What was the degree of sampling bias and non-response bias in the information gathered? (x) What was the degree of misrepresentation by respondents? (xi) How properly was the information by respondents? (xii) Was statistical analysis properly applied?

MARKET SURVEY

Secondary information, though useful, often does not provide a comprehensive basis for demand and market analysis. It needs to be supplemented with primary information gathered through a market survey, specific for the project being appraised.The market survey may be a census survey or a sample survey. In a census survey the entire population is covered. (The word 'population' is used here in a particular sense. It refers to the totality of all units under consideration in a specific study. Examples are- all industries using milling machines, all readers of the *Economic Times*). Census surveys are employed principally for intermediate goods and investment goods when such goods are used by a small number of firms. In other cases, a census survey is prohibitively costly and may also be infeasible. For example, it would be inordinately expensive to cover every user of Lifebuoy or every person in the income bracket Rs. 10,000-Rs. 15,000. Due to the above mentioned limitations of the census survey, the market survey, in practice, is typically a sample survey. In such a survey a sample of the population is contacted/observed and relevant information is gathered. On the basis of such information, inferences about the population may be drawn. The information sought in a market survey may relate to one or more of the following (i) Total demand and rate of growth of demand; (ii) Demand in different segments of the market; (iii) Income and price elasticity of demand; (iv) Motives for buying; (v) Purchasing plans and intentions; (vi) Satisfaction with existing products; (vii) Unsatisfied needs; (viii) Attitudes toward various products (ix) Distributive trade practices and preferences; (x) Socio-economic characteristics of buyers.

Steps in a sample survey

Typically, a sample survey consists of the following steps:

1. Definition of the target population— In defining the target population the important terms should be carefully and unambiguously defined. The target population may be divided into various segments which may have differing characteristics. For example, all television owners may be divided into three to four income brackets.

2. Selection of sampling scheme and sample size— There are several sampling schemes- simple random sampling, cluster sampling, sequential sampling, stratified sampling, systematic sampling, and nonprobability sampling. Each scheme has its advantages and limitations.The sample size, other things being equal, has a bearing on the reliability of the estimates— the larger the sample size, the greater the reliability.

3. Preparation of the questionnaire— The questionnaire is the principal instrument for eliciting information from the sample of the respondents. The effectiveness of the questionnaire as a device for eliciting the desired information depends on its length, the types of questions, and the wording of questions. Developing the questionnaire requires thorough understanding of the product/service and its usage, imagination, insights into human behaviour, appreciation of subtle linguistic nuances, and familiarity with the tools of descriptive and inferential statistics to be used later for analysis. It also requires knowledge of psychological scaling techniques if the same are employed for obtaining information relating to attitudes, motivations, and psychological traits. Industry and trade market surveys, in comparison to consumer surveys, generally involve more technical and specialized questions. Since the quality of the questionnaire has an important bearing on the results of market survey, the questionnaire should be tried out in a pilot survey and modified in the light of problems/difficulties noted.

4. Recruiting and training of field investigators must be planned well since it can be time-consuming. Great care must be taken for recruiting the right kinds of investigators and imparting the proper kind of training to them. Investigators involved in industry and trade market survey need intimate knowledge of the product and technical background particularly for products based on sophisticated technologies.

5. Obtaining information as per the questionnaire from the sample of respondents— Respondents may be interviewed personally, telephonically or by mail for obtaining information. Personal interviews ensure a high rate of response. They are, however, expensive and likely to result in biased responses because of the presence of the interviewer. Mail surveys are economical and evoke fairly candid responses. The response rate, however, is often low. Telephonic interviews, common in western countries, have very limited applicability in India because telephone tariffs are high and telephone connections few.

6. Scrutiny of information gathered— Information gathered should be thoroughly scrutinized to eliminate data which is internally inconsistent and which is of dubious validity. For example, a respondent with a high income and large family may say that he lives in a one-room tenement. Such information, probably inaccurate, should be deleted. Sometimes data inconsistencies may be revealed only after some analysis.

7. Analysis and interpretation of data— Data gathered in the survey needs to be analysed and interpreted with care and imagination. After tabulating it as per a plan of analysis, suitable statistical investigation may be conducted, wherever possible and necessary. For purposes of statistical analysis, a variety of methods are available. They may be divided into two broad categories: parametric methods and nonparametric methods. Parametric methods assume that the variable or attribute under study conforms to some known distribution. Nonparametric methods do not presuppose any particular distribution.

Results of data based on sample survey will have to be extrapolated for the target population. For this purpose, appropriate inflatory factors,based on the ratio of the size of the target population and the size of the sample studied, will have be to be used. The statistical analysis of data should be directed by a person who has a good background in statistics as well as economics. It may be emphasized that the results of the market survey can be vitiated by- (i) non-representativeness of the sample, (ii) imprecision and inadequacies in the questions, (iii) failure of the respondents to comprehend the questions, (iv) deliberate distortions in the answers given by the respondents, (v) inept handling of the interviews by the investigators, (vi) cheating on the part of the investigators, (vii) slipshod scrutiny of data, and (viii) incorrect and inappropriate analysis and interpretation of data.

DEMAND FORECASTING

After gathering information about various aspects of the market and demand from primary and secondary sources, an attempt may be made to estimate future demand. Several methods are available for demand forecasting. The important ones are—

(i) Trend projection method

It consists of (i) determining the trend of consumption by analyzing past consumption statistics, and (ii) projecting future consumption by extrapolating the trend.

The trend of consumption may be represented by one of the following relationships:

Linear Relationship: $Y_t = a + bt$ ... (1)

Exponential Relationship: $Y_t = ae^{bt}$ ... (2)

On logarithmic transformation this becomes:

$\log Y_t = \log a + bt$

Polynomial Relationship: $Y_t = a_0 + a_1t + a_2t^2 + \ldots + a_nt^n$ ... (3)

Cobb Douglas Relationship: $Y_t = at^b$ ... (4)

On logarithmic transformation this becomes:

$$\log Y_t = \log a + b \log t$$

In the above equations Yt represents demand for year t, t is the time variable, a, b and aj's are constants.

Out of the above relationships the most commonly used relationship is-

$$Yt = a + bt$$

This relationship may be estimated by using one of the following methods: (i) visual curve fitting method, and (ii) least squares method. *Evaluation*— The basic assumption underlying the trend projection method is that the factors which influenced the behaviour of consumption in the past would continue to influence the behaviour of consumption in the future. This hypothesis is sometimes referred to as the hypothesis of "mutually compensating effects". Clearly, this is a deterministic hypothesis of questionable validity. Notwithstanding this weakness, the trend projection method is used popularly in practice. Often a starting point in the forecasting exercise, it is likely to be relied upon heavily when no other viable method seems available. The ease with which it can be applied may induce a sense of complacency.

(ii) Consumption level method

Useful for a product which is directly consumed, this method estimates consumption level on the basis of elasticity coefficients, the important ones being the income elasticity of demand and the price elasticity of demand.

Income elasticity of demand— The income elasticity of demand reflects the responsiveness of demand to variations in income. It is measured as follows:

$$E_1 = \frac{Q_2 - Q_1}{I_2 - I_1} \times \frac{I_1 + I_2}{Q_2 + Q_1}$$

Where E_1 = income elasticity of demand

    Q_1 = quantity demanded in the base year

    Q_2 = quantity demanded in the following year

    I_1 = income level in the base year

    I_2 = income level in the following year

Example— The following information is available on quantity demanded and income level: Q_1 = 50, Q_2 = 55, I_1 = 1,000, and I_2 = 1,020. The income elasticity of demand is-

$$E_1 = \frac{55 - 50}{1{,}020 - 1{,}000} \times \frac{1{,}000 + 1{,}020}{55 + 50} = 4.81$$

The information on income elasticity of demand along with projected income may be used to obtain a demand forecast. To illustrate, suppose the present per capita annual demand for paper is 1 kg and the present per capita annual income is Rs. 1,2000. The income elasticity of demand for paper is 2. The projected per capita annual income three years hence is expected to be 10 per cent higher than what it is now. The projected per capita demand for paper three years hence will be-

$$\left(\begin{array}{c} \text{Present per} \\ \text{capita income} \end{array}\right) \left(\begin{array}{c} 1 + \text{per capital change} \\ \text{in income level} \end{array} \quad \begin{array}{c} \text{income elasticity} \\ \text{of demand} \end{array}\right)$$

$$= (1)\,(1 + 0.10 \times 2) = 1.2 \text{ kg.}$$

The aggregate demand projection for paper will simply be-

Projected per capita demand × Projected population

The income elasticity of demand differs from one product to another. Further, for a given product, it tends to vary from one income group to another and from one region to another. Hence, wherever possible, disaggregative analysis should be attempted.

Price elasticity of demand— The price elasticity of demand measures the responsiveness of demand to variations in price. It is defined as—

$$E_p = \frac{Q_2 - Q_1}{P_2 - P_1} \times \frac{P_1 + P_2}{Q_2 + Q_1}$$

Where, Ep = price elasticity of demand

       Q1 = quantity demanded in the base year

       Q2 quantity demanded in the following year

       P1 = price per unit in the base year

       P2 = price per unit in the following year

Example— The following information is available about a certain product:

       P1 = Rs. 600, Q1 = 10,000, P2 = Rs. 800, Q2 = 9,000. The price elasticity of demand is:

$$E_p = \frac{9000 - 10{,}000}{800 - 500} \times \frac{600 + 800}{9{,}000 + 10{,}000} = -0.37$$

The price elasticity of demand is a useful tool in demand analysis. The future volume of demand may be estimated on the basis of the price elasticity coefficient and expected price change. The price elasticity coefficient may also be used to study the impact of variable price that may obtain in future on the economic viability of the project. In using the price elasticity measure, however, the following considerations should be borne in mind: (i) the price elasticity coefficient is applicable to only small variations. (ii) The price elasticity measure is based on the assumption that the structure and behaviour remain constant.

(iii) End use method

Suitable for estimating the demand for intermediate products, the end use method, also referred to as the consumption coefficient method involves the following steps:

1. Identify the possible uses of the product.

2. Define the consumption coefficient of the product for various uses.

3. Project the output levels for the consuming industries.

4. Derive the demand for the product.

This method may be illustrated with an example. A certain industrial chemical is used by four industries, Alpha, Beta, Gamma, and Kappa. The consumption coefficients for these industries,the projected output levels for these industries for the year X, and the projected demand are shown in Exhibit 1.

Projected Demand

	Consumption coefficient*	Projected output in Year X	Projected demand in Year X
Alpha	2.0	10,000	20,000
Beta	1.2	15,000	18,000
Kappa	0.8	20,000	16,000
Gamma	0.5	30,000	15,000

*This is expressed in tones per unit of output of the consuming industry.

As is clear from the foregoing discussion, the key inputs required for the application of the end-use method are— (i) projected output levels ofconsuming industries (units), and (ii) consumption coefficients. It may be difficult to estimate the projected output levels of consuming industries (units). More important, the consumption coefficients may vary from one period to another in the wake of technological changes and improvements in the methods of manufacturing. Hence, the end-use method should be used judiciously.

(iv) Leading Indicator Method

Leading indicators are variables which change ahead of other variables, the lagging variables. Hence, observed changes in leading indicators may be used to predict the changes in lagging variables. For example, the change in the level of urbanization a leading indicator may be used to predict the change in the demand for air conditioners a lagging variable.

Two basic steps are involved in using the leading indicator method: (i) First, identify the appropriate leading indicator(s). (ii) Second, establish the relationship between the leading indicator(s) and the variable to be forecast.

The principal merit of this method is that it does not require a forecast of an explanatory variable. It, however, is characterized by certain problems. (i) It may be difficult to find an appropriate leading indicator(s). (ii) The lead-lag relationship may not remain stable over time. In view of these problems this method has limited use.

(v) Econometric method

An econometric model is a mathematical representation of economic relationship/s derived from economic theory. The primary objective of econometric analysis is to forecast the future behaviour of the economic variables incorporated in the model. Two types of econometric models are employed: the single equation model and the simultaneous equation model. The single equation model assumes that one variable, the dependent variable (also referred to as the explained variable), is influenced by one or more independent variables (also referred to as the explanatory variables). In other words, one-way causality is postulated. An example of the single equation model is given below:

$$D_t = a_0 + a_1 P_t + a_2 N_t$$

Where, D_t = demand for a certain product in year t

P_t = price for the product in year t

N_t = income in year t

The simultaneous equation model portrays economic relationships in terms of two or more equations. Consider a highly simplified three equation econometric model of Indian economy.

$$GNP_t = G_t + I_t + C_t \dots (5)$$

$$I_t = a_0 + a_1 GNP_t \dots (6)$$

$$C_t = b_0 + b_1 GNP_t \dots (7)$$

Where GNP_t = gross national product for year t

G_t = governmental purchases for year t

I_t = gross investment for year t

C_t = consumption for year t

In the above model, Eq. (5) is just a definitional equation which says that the gross national product is equal to the sum of government purchases, gross investment and consumption. Eq. (6) postulates that investment is a linear function of gross national product; Eq. (7) posits that consumption is a linear function of gross national product. The construction and use of an econometric model involves four broad steps.

1. *Specification*— This refers to the expression of an economic relationship in mathematical form. Equation (6), for example, posits that investments is a linear function of gross national product.
2. *Estimation*— This involves the determination of the parameter values and other statistics by a suitable method. The principal methods of estimation are the least squares method and the maximum likelihood method, the former being the most popular method in practice.
3. *Verification*— This step is concerned with accepting or rejecting the specification as a reasonable approximation to truth on the basis of the results of estimation and appropriate statistical tests applied to them.
4. *Prediction*— This involves projection of the value of the explained variable(s).

Evaluation— The econometric method offers certain advantages- (i) The process of econometric analysis sharpens the understanding of complex cause-effect relationships, (ii) the econometric model provides a basis for testing assumptions and for judging how sensitive the results are to changes in assumptions. The limitations of the econometric method are— (i) it is expensive and data-demanding. (ii) to forecast the behaviour of the dependent variable, one needs the projected values of independent variable (s). The difficulty in obtaining these may be the main limiting factor in employing econometric method for forecasting purposes.

Market penetration for the product— Once a reasonably good handle over the aggregate demand is obtained, the next logical question is: What will be the likely demand for the product of the project under examination? The answer to this question depends on—

1. Aggregate potential supply
2. Nature of competition
3. Consumer preferences
4. Sales promotion efforts

If the aggregate potential domestic supply is likely to be significantly less than the aggregate potential domestic demand, the demand for the product of the project under examination is likely to be very strong, provided liberal imports which may hurt domestic manufacturers are not allowed. The nature of competition and market-sharing arrangement (if any) has a bearing on the demand for the product of the project under examination. Consumer preferences for competing products and the sales promotional efforts of various competitors obviously influence the relative market shares enjoyed by them.

UNCERTAINTIES IN DEMAND FORECASTING
Demand forecasts are subject to error and uncertainty which arise from three principal sources:
(i) Data about past and present market
The analysis of past and present market, which serves as the springboard for the projection exercise, may be vitiated by the following inadequacies of data:
Lack of standardization— Data pertaining to market features like product, price, quantity, cost, income etc. may not reflect uniform concepts and measures.
Few observations— Not enough observations may be available to conduct meaningful analysis.
Influence of abnormal factors— Some of the observations may be influenced by abnormal factors like war or natural calamity.
(ii) Methods of forecasting
Methods used for demand forecasting are characterized by limitations.*Inability to handle unquantifiable factors*— Most of the forecasting methods, quantitative in nature, cannot handle unquantifiable factors which sometimes can be of immense significance.
Unrealistic assumptions— Each forecasting method is based on certain assumptions. For example, the trend projection method is based on the 'mutually compensation effects' premise and the end-use method is based on the constancy of technical coefficients. Uncertainty arises when the assumptions underlying the chosen method tend to be unrealistic and erroneous.
Excessive data requirement— In general, the more advanced a method, the greater the data requirement. For example, to use an econometric model one has to forecast the future values of explanatory variables in order to project the explained variable. Clearly, predicting the future value of explanatory variables is a difficult and uncertain exercise.
(iii) Environmental changes
The environment in which a business functions is characterized by numerous uncertainties. The important sources of uncertainty are mentioned below:
Technological change— This is a very important but hard-to-predict factor which influences business prospects. A technological advancement may create a new product which performs the same function more efficiently and economically, thereby cutting into the market for the existing product. For example, electronic watches have encroached on the market for mechanical watches.
Shift in governmental policy— In India, governmental regulation of business is extensive. Changes in governmental policy, which may be difficult to anticipate, may have a telling effect on business environment, e.g. granting of licenses to new companies, particularly foreign companies, may alter the market situation significantly.; banning the import of a certain product may create a sheltered market for the existing producers; liberalizing the import of some product may lead to stiff competition in the market place; relaxation of price and distribution controls may widen the market considerably.

Developments on the international scene— Developments on the international scene may have a profound effect on industries. The most classic example of recent times is the OPEC price hike, which led to nearstagnation in the Indian automobile industry.

Discovery of new sources of raw material— Discovery of new sources of raw materials, particularly hydrocarbons, can have a significant impact on the market situation of several products.

Vagaries of monsoon— Monsoon, which plays an important role in the Indian economy, is somewhat unpredictable. The behaviour of monsoon influences, directly or indirectly, the demand for a wise range of products.

COPING WITH UNCERTAINTIES

Given the uncertainties in demand forecasting, adequate efforts, along the following lines may be made to cope with uncertainties.

1. Conduct analysis with data based on uniform and standard definitions.
2. In identifying trends, coefficients, and relationships, ignore the abnormal or out-of-the-ordinary observations.
3 Critically evaluate the assumptions of the forecasting methods and choose a method which is appropriate to the situation.
4. Adjust the projections derived from quantitative analysis in the light of a due consideration of unquantifiable, but significant influences.
5. Monitor the environment imaginatively to identify important changes.
6. Consider likely alternative scenarios and their impact on market and competition.
7. Conduct sensitivity analysis to assess the impact on the size of demand for unfavorable and favourable variations of the determining factors from their most likely levels.

TECHNICAL ANALYSIS

The success of an enterprise depends upon the entrepreneur doing the right thing at the right time. Starting a new venture is a very challenging and rewarding task. A businessman has to take numerous decisions, right from the conception of a business idea, upon the start of production. Hence, the identification of the project to be undertaken, requires an analysis of the project in depth. Therefore, a technical and financial analysis of the project has to be undertaken.

TECHNICAL ANALYSIS

Analysis of technical and engineering aspects is done continually when a project is being examined and formulated. Other types of analyses are dependent and closely intertwined with technical analysis. Technical analysis is concerned primarily with:

Materials and inputs

An important aspect of technical appraisal is concerned with defining the materials and inputs required, specifying their properties in some detail, and setting up their supply programme. There is an intimate relationship between the study of materials and inputs and other aspects of project formulation, particularly those concerned with location, technology, and equipment. Materials and inputs may be classified into four broad categories: (i) raw materials, (ii) processed industrial materials and components, (iii) auxiliary materials and factory supplies, and (iv) utilities.

(i) Raw materials— Raw materials (processed and /or semiprocessed) may be classified into four types: (i) agricultural products, (ii) mineral products, (iii) livestock and forest products, and (iv) marine products.

(ii) Processed industrial materials and components— Processed industrial materials and components (base metals, semi-processed materials, manufactured parts, components, and sub-assembly represent an important input for a number of industries. In studying them the following questions need to be answered: In the case of industrial materials, what are their properties? What is the total requirement of the project? What quantity would be available from domestic source? What quantity would be available from foreign sources? How dependable are the supplies? What has been the past trend in prices? What is the likely future behaviour of prices?

(iii) Auxiliary materials and factory supplies— In addition to the basic raw materials and processed industrial materials and components, a manufacturing project requires various auxiliary materials and factory supplies, like chemicals, additives, packaging materials, paints, varnishes, oils, grease, cleaning materials, etc.The requirements of such auxiliary materials and supplies should be taken into account in the feasibility study.

(iv) Utilities— A broad assessment of utilizes (power, water, steam, fuel, etc.) may be made at the time of input study though a detailed assessment can be made only after formulating the project with respect to location, technology, and plant selection. Since the successful operation of a project critically depends on adequate availability of utilities the following points should be raised whiled conducting the input study: What quantities are required? What are the sources of supply? What would be the potential availability? What are the likely shortages/bottlenecks? What measures may be taken to augment supplies.

Production technology

For manufacturing a product/service often two or more alternative technologies are available. For example:

- Steel can be made either by the Bessemer process or the open hearth process.
- Cement can be made either by the dry process or the wet process.
- Soda can be made by the electrolysis method or the chemical method.
- Paper, using bagasse as the raw material, can be manufactured by the kraft process or the soda process or the simon cusi process.
- Vinyl chloride can be manufactured by using one of the following reactions: acetylene on hydrochloric acid or ethylene or chlorine.

Choice of technology

The choice of technology is influenced by a variety of considerations:

(i) Principal inputs— The choice of technology depends on the principal inputs available for the project. In some cases, the raw materials available influences the technology chosen. For example, the quality of limestones determines whether the wet or dry process should be used for a cement plant. It may be emphasized that a technology based on indigenous inputs may be preferable to one based on imported inputs because of uncertainties characterizing imports, particularly in a country like India.

(ii) Investment outlay and production cost— The effect of alternative technologies of investment outlay and production cost over a period of time should be carefully assessed.

(iii) Use by other units— The technology adopted must be proven by successful use by other units, preferably in India.

(iv) Product mix— The technology chosen must be judged in terms of the total product-mix generated by it, including saleable byproducts.

(v) Latest developments— The technology adopted must be based on latest development in order to ensure that the likelihood of technological obsolescence in the near future, at least, is minimized.

(vi) Ease of absorption— The ease with which a particular technology can be absorbed can influence the choice of technology. Sometimes a high-level technology may be beyond the absorptive capacity of a developing country which may lack trained personnel to handle that technology.

Product Mix

The choice of product mix is guided primarily by market requirements. In the production of most of the items variations in size and quality are aimed the production of most of the items, variations in size and quality are aimed at satisfying a broad range of customers. For example, production of shoes to different customers. It may be noted that sometimes slight variations in quality can enable a company to expand its market and enjoy higher profitability. For example, a toilet soap manufacturing unit may by minor variation in raw material, packaging,and sales promotion offer a high profit margin soap to consumers in upper-income brackets.

While planning the production facilities of the firm, some flexibility with respect to the product mix must be sought. Such flexibility enables the firm to alter its product mix in response to changing market conditions and enhances the power of the firm to survive and grow under different situations. The degree of flexibility chosen may be based on a careful analysis of the additional investment requirements for different degrees of flexibility.

Plant capacity

Plant capacity (also referred to as production as capacity) refers to the volume or number of units that can be manufactured during a given period. Several factors have a bearing on the capacity decision.

(i) Technological requirement— For many industrial projects, particularly in process type industries, there is a certain minimum economic size determined by the technological factor. For example, a cement plant should have a capacity of at least 300 tonnes per day in order to use the rotary kiln method; otherwise, it has to employ the vertical shaft method which is suitable for lower capacity.

(ii) Input constraints— In a developing country like India, there may be constraints on the availability of certain inputs. Power supply may be limited; basic raw materials may be scarce; foreign exchange available for imports may be inadequate. Constraints of these kinds should be borne in mind while choosing the plant capacity.

(iii) Investment cost— When serious input constraints do not obtain, the relationship between capacity and investment cost is an important consideration. Typically, the investment cost per unit of capacity decreases as the plant capacity increases. This relationship may be expressed as follows:

Where C_1 = derived cost for Q_1 units of capacity

         C_2 = known cost for Q_2 units of capacity

         α = a factor reflecting capacity-cost relationship. This is usually between 0.2 and 0.9.

(iv) Market conditions— The anticipated market for the product/service has an important bearing on plant capacity. If the market for the product is likely to be very strong, a plant of higher capacity is preferable. If the market is likely to be uncertain, it might be advantageous to start with a smaller capacity. If the market, starting from a small base, is expected to grow rapidly, the initial capacity may be higher than the initial level of demand further additions to capacity may be affected with the growth of market.

(v) Resources of the firm— The resources, both managerial and financial, available to a firm define a limit on its capacity decision. Obviously, a firm cannot choose a scale of operations beyond its financial resources and managerial capability.

(vi) Governmental policy— The capacity level may be constrained by governmental policy. Given the level of additional capacity to be created in an industry, within the licensing framework of the government the government may decide to distribute the additional capacity among several firms.

Location and site

The choice of location and site follows an assessment of demand, size, and input requirement. Though often used synonymously, the terms 'location' and 'site' should be distinguished. Location refers to a fairly broad area like a city, an industrial zone, or a coastal area; site refers to a specific piece of land where the project would be set up.

The choice of location is influenced by a variety of considerations: proximity to raw materials and markets, availability of infrastructure, governmental policies, and other factors.

(i) Proximity to raw materials and markets— An important consideration for location is the proximity to sources of raw materials and nearness to the market for final products. In terms of a basic locational model, the optimal location is one where the total cost (raw material transportation cost plus production cost plus distribution cost for final product) is minimized. This generally implies that: (i) a resource-based project like a cement plant or a steel mill should be located close the source of basic material (for example, limestone in the case of a cement plant and iron-ore in the case of a steel plant); (ii) a project based on imported material may be located near a port; and (iii) a project manufacturing a perishable product should be close to the center of consumption. However, for many industrial products proximity to the source of raw material or the center of consumption may not be very important. Petro-chemical units or refineries, for example, may be located close to the source of raw material, or close to the center of consumption, or at some intermediate point.

(ii) Availability of infrastructure— Availability of power,transportation, water, and communications should be carefully assessed before a location decision is made. Adequate supply of power is a very important condition for location— insufficient power can be a major constraint, particularly in the case of an electricity-intensive project like an aluminium plant. In evaluating power supply the following should be looked into: the quantum of power available, the stability of power supply, the structure of power tariff, and the investment required by the project for a tie-up in the network of the power supplying agency. For transporting the inputs of the project and distributing the outputs of the project, adequate transport connections— whether by rail, road, sea, inland water, or air— are reqired. The availability, reliability and cost of transportation for various alternative locations should be assessed.Given the plant capacity and the type of technology, the water requirement for the project can be assessed. Once the required quantity is estimated, the amount to be drawn from the public utility system and the amount to be provided by the project from surface or sub-surface sources may be determined. For doing this the following factors may be examined: relative costs, relative dependabilities, and relative qualities.

In addition to power, transport, and water, the project should have adequate communication facilities like telephone and fax etc.

(iii) Governmental policies— Governmental policies have a bearing on location. In the case of public sector projects, location is directly decided by the government. It may be based on a wider policy for regional dispersion of industries.In the case of private sector projects, location is influenced by certain governmental restrictions and inducements. The government may prohibit the setting up of industrial projects in certain areas which suffer from urban congestion. More positively, the government offers inducements for establishing industries in backward areas. These inducements consist of outright subsidies, concessional finance, tax relief, and other benefits.

(iv) Other factors— Several other factors have to be assessed before reaching a location decision: ease in coping with environmental pollution, labour situation, climatic conditions, and general living conditions. A project may cause environmental pollution in various ways: it may throw gaseous emission; it may produce liquid and solid discharges; it may cause noise, heat, and vibrations. The location study should analyse the costs of mitigating environmental pollution to tolerable levels at alternative locations.

The labour situation at alternative locations may be assessed in terms of: (i) the availability of labour, skilled, semi-skilled, and unskilled; (ii) the past trends in labour rates, the prevailing labour rates, and the projected labour rates; and (iii) the state of industrial relations judged in terms of the frequency and severity of strikes and lockouts and the attitudes of labour and management. The climatic conditions (like temperature, humidity, wind, sunshine, rainfall, snowfall, dust and fumes, flooding, and earthquakes) have an important influence on location. They have a bearing on cost as they determine the extent of air-conditioning, de-humidification, refrigeration, special drainage, etc., required for the project.

General living conditions, judged in terms of cost of living, housing situation, and facilities for education, recreation, transport, and medical care, need to be assessed at alternative locations.

Machinery and equipment

The requirement of machinery and equipment is dependent on production technology and plant capacity. It is also influenced by the type of project. For a process-oriented industry, like a petrochemical unit, machinery and equipment required should be such that the various
stages have to be matched well. The choice of machinery and equipment for a manufacturing industry is somewhat wider as various machines can perform the same function with varying degrees of accuracy. For example, the configuration of machines required for the manufacture of refrigerators could take various forms. To determine the kinds of machinery and equipment requirement for a manufacturing industry, the following procedure may be followed: (i) Estimate the likely levels of production over time. (ii) Define the various machining and otheroperations. (iii) Calculate the machine hours required for each type of operation. (iv) Select machinery and equipment required for each function. The equipment required for the project may be classified into the following types: (i) plant (process) equipment, (ii) mechanical equipment, (iii) electrical equipment, (iv) instruments, (v) controls, (vi) internal transportation system, and (vii) other machinery and equipment. In addition to the machinery and equipment, a list should be prepared of spare parts and tools required. This may be divided into: (i) spare parts and tools to be purchased with original equipment, and (ii) spare parts and tools required for operational wear and tear.

Constraints in selecting machinery and equipment— In selecting the machinery and equipment, certain constraints should be borne in mind:

(i) there may be a limited availability of power to set up an electricity intensive plant like, for example, a large electric furnace; (ii) there may be difficulty in transporting a heavy equipment to a remote location; (iii) workers may not be able to operate, at least in the initial periods, certain sophisticated equipment such as numerically controlled machines; (iv) the import policy of the government may preclude the import of certain types of machinery and equipment.

Structures and civil works

Structures and civil works may be divided into three categories: (i) site preparation and development, (ii) buildings and structures, and (iii) outdoor works.

(i) Site preparation and development— This covers the following: (i) grading and leveling of the site, (ii) demolition and removal of existing structures, (iii) relocation of existing pipelines cables,roads, powerlines, etc., (iv) reclamation of swamps, draining and removal of standing water, (v) connections for the following utilities from the site to the public network: electric power (high tension and low tension), water (use water and drinking water), communications (telephone, fax, etc.), roads, railway sidings, and (vi) other site preparation and developmental work.

(ii) Buildings— Buildings and structures may be divided into: (i) factory or process buildings; (ii) ancillary buildings required for stores, warehouses, laboratories, utility supply centers, maintenance services, and others; (iii) administrative buildings; (iv) staff welfare buildings, cafetaria, and medical service buildings; and (v) residential buildings.

(iii) Outdoor works— Outdoor works cover (i) supply and distribution of utilities (water, electric power, communication, steam and gas); (ii) handling and treatment of emissions, wastages, and effluents; (iii) transportation and traffic arrangements (roads, railway tracks, paths, parking areas, sheds, garages, traffic signals, etc.): (iv) outdoor lighting; (v) landscaping; and (vi) enclosure and supervision (boundary wall, fencing, barriers, gates, doors, security posts, etc.).

Project charts and layouts

Once data is available on the principal dimension of the project— market size, plant capacity, required technology, equipment and civil works, conditions obtaining at plant site, and supply of inputs to the project— project charts and layouts may be prepared. These define the scope of the project and provide the basis for detailed project engineering and estimation of investment and production costs.

Work Schedule

The work schedule, as its name suggests, reflects the plan of work concerning installation as well as initial operation. The purpose of the work schedule is:

 - To anticipate problems likely to arise during the installation phase and suggest possible means for coping with them.
 - To establish the phasing of investments taking into account availability of finances.
 - To develop a plant of operations covering the initial period (the running in period).

Often, it is found that the required inputs like raw material and power are not available in adequate quantity when the plant is ready for commissioning, or the plant is not ready when the raw material arrives.

UNIT III

INTRODUCTION

The efficient allocation of funds is among the main functions of financial management. Allocation of funds means investment of funds in assets or activities. It is also called investment decision because we have to select the assests in which investment has to be made. These assets can be classified into two parts :-
i) Short-term or Current Assets.
ii) Long-term or Fixed Assets

INVESTMENT APPRAISAL DECISION

Investment appraisal is a way that a business will assess the attractiveness of possible investments or projects based on the findings of several different capital budgeting and financing techniques. For traders, it is a form of fundamental analysis as it can help identify long-term trends as well as a company's perceived profitability.

MEANING AND FEATURES OF INVESTMENT APPRAISAL OR CAPITAL EXPENDITURE

A investment appraisal decision may be defined as the firm's decision to invest its current funds most efficiently in the long-term assets in anticipation of an expected flow of benefits over a series of years. In other words, "capital budgeting is used to evaluate the expenditure decisions such as acquisition of fixed assets, changes in old assets and their replacement." Activities such as change in the method of sales distribution or undertaking an advertisement campaign or a research and development programme have long-term implication for the firm's expenditure and benefits and therefore, they may also be evaluated as investment decisions.

Features of Investment Appraisal/ Capital Budgeting Decisions

Following are the features of investment decisions

- ➢ Investment of fund is made in long-term assets.
- ➢ The exchange of current funds for future benefits.
- ➢ Future profits accrue to the firm over several years.

These decisions are more risky. It is significant to emphasize that expenditure and benefits of an investment should be measured in cash. In the investment analysis, it is cash flow which is important, not the accounting profit. It may also be pointed out that investment decisions affect the firm's value. The firm's value will increase if investment are profitable. Investment should be evaluated on the basis of a criteria on which it is compatible with the objective of the shareholder's wealth maximisation. An investment will add to the shareholder's wealth if it yields benefits in excess of the minimum benefits as per the opportunity cost of capital.

IMPORTANCE OF INVESTMENT APPRAISAL /CAPITAL EXPENDITURE DECISION

Investment decisions require special attention because of the following reasons :

1. Growth :- The effects of investment decisions extend into the future and have to endured for a longer period than the consequences of the current operating expenditure. A firm's decisions to invest in long-term assets has a decisive influence on the rate direction of its growth. A wrong decisions can prove disastrous for the continued survival of the firm.

2. Risk :- A long-term commitment of funds may also change the risk complexity of the firm. If the adoption of an investment increases average gain but causes frequent fluctuations in its earnings, the firm will become very risky.

3. Funding :- Investment decisions generally involve large amount of funds. Funds are scarce resource in our country. Hence the capital budgeting decision is very important.

4. Irreversibility :- Most investment decisions are irreversible

5. Complexity :- Investment decisions are among the firm's most difficult decisions. They are concerned with assessment of future events which are difficult to predict. It is really a complex problem to correctly estimate the future cash flow of investment.

Objectives of Investment Appraisal/Capital Budgeting Decision

Capital budgeting helps in selection of profitable projects. A company should have system for estimating cash flow of projects. A multidisciplinary team of managers should be assigned the task of developing cash flow estimates. Once cash flow have been estimated, projects should be evaluated to determine their profitability. Evaluations criteria chosen should correctly rank the projects. Once the projects have been selected they should be monitored and controlled. Proper authority should exist for capital spending. Critical projects involving large sum of money may be supervised by the top management. A company should have a sound capital budgeting and reporting system for this purpose. Based on the comparison of actual and expected performance, projects should be reappraised and remedial action should be taken.

2.5 INVESTMENT APPRAISAL /CAPITAL BUDGETING PROCESS

Investment apopraisal/Capital budgeting is a complex process which may be divided into five broad phases.These are :-

- ➢ Planning
- ➢ Analysis
- ➢ Selection
- ➢ Implementation
- ➢ Review

Planning

The planning phase of a firm's capital budgeting process is concerned with the articulation of its broad strategy and the generation and preliminary screening of project proposals. This provides the framework which shapes, guides and circumscribes the identification of individual project opportunities.

Analysis

The focus of this phase of capital budgeting is on gathering, preparing and summarizing relevant information about various project proposals which are being considered for inclusion in the capital budget. Under this a detail analysis of the marketing, technical, economic and ecological aspects in undertaken.

Selection

Project would be selected in the order in which they are ranked and cut off point would be reached when the cumulative total cost of the projects become equal to the size of the plan funds. A wide range of appraisal criteria have been suggested for selection of a project. They are divided into two categories viz, non-discounting criteria and discounting criteria.

Techniques for Investment Appraisal

There are two broad criteria of investment appraisal :

1. Non discounting criteria

The method of investment appraisal are the techniques which are used to make comparative evaluation of profitability of investment.The non-discounting methods of capital are as follows :

• Pay back period method (PBP)

• Accounting rate of return method (ARR)

2. Discounting Criteria

• Net present value method (NPV)

• Internal rate of return method (IRR)

• profitability index method (PVI)

Non-discounting criteria

Pay back period method : Under this method the pay back period of each project investment proposal is calculated. The investment proposal which has the least payback period is considered profitable. Actual pay back is compared with the standardone if actual pay back period is less than the standard the project will be accepted and in case, actual payback period is more than the standard payback period, the project will be rejected. So, pay back period is the number of years required for the original investment to be recouped. For example, if the investment required for a project is Rs. 20,000 and it is likely to generate cash flow of Rs. 10,000 for 5 years. Pay back Period will be 2 years. It means that investment will be recovered in first 2 years of the project. Method of calculating payback period is

$$PB = \frac{Investment}{Annual\ Cash\ in\ Flow}$$

Accounting Rate of Return : This method is also called average rate of return method. This method is based on accounting information rather than cash flows. It can be calculated as -

$$ARR = \frac{Average\ annual\ profit\ after\ taxes}{Average\ Investment} \times 100$$

$$\frac{Total\ of\ after\ but\ profit\ it\ of\ all\ the\ years}{Number\ of\ years}$$

$$Average\ Investment = \frac{Original\ Investment + Salvage\ value}{2}$$

Discounted Criteria

Under these methods the projected future cash flows are discounted by a certain rate called cost of capital. The second main feature of these methods is that they take into account all the benefits and costs accruing during the life time of the project. Discounted cash flow method are briefly described as follow :-

Net Present Value Method (NPV) : In this method present value of cash flow is calculated for which cash flows are discounted. The rate of discount is called cost of capital and is equal to the minimum rate of return which must accrue from the project. NPV is the difference between present value of cash inflows and present value of cash outflows. NPV can be calculated as under :-

$$NPV = \frac{CF_1}{(1+K)_1} + \frac{CF_2}{(1+K)_2} + \frac{CF_3}{(1+K)_3} + \ldots\ldots\ldots + \frac{CF_n}{(1+K)_n} - C$$

Where Cf1, Cf2……………………………… represent cash inflows, k is the firm's cost of capital, C is cost outlay of the investment proposal and n, is the expected life of the proposal. If the project has salvage value also it should be added in the cash inflow of the last year. Similarly, if some working capital is also needed it will be added to the initial cost of the project and to the cash flow's of the last year. If the NPV of a project is more than zero, the project should be accepted and if NPV is less than zero it should be rejected. When NPV of two more projects under consideration is more than zero, the project whose NPV is the highest should be accepted.

Internal rate of return method (IRR) : Under this method initial cost and annual cash inflows are given. The unknown rate of return is ascertained. In other words "The internal rate of return is that rate which equates the present value of cash inflows with the present value of cash outflows of an investment project." At the internal rate of return NPV of a project is zero. Like NPV method IRR method also considers time value of money. In IRR method, the discount rate (r) depends upon initial investment expenditure and the future cash inflows. IRR is calculated as follows :

$$C = \frac{A_1}{(1+r)^1} + \frac{A_2}{(1+r)^2} + \frac{A_3}{(1+r)^3} + \ldots\ldots + \frac{A_n}{(1+r)^n}$$

C = initial cash outflow
n = number of years
r = rate of return which is to be calculated
A_1 A_2 A_3……………… A_n are cash inflows in various years.

Profitability index/ Benefit-cost ratio : It is the ratio of value of future cash benefits discounted at some required rate of return to the initial cash outflows of the investment PI method should be adopted when the initial costs of projects are different. NPV method is considered good when the initial cost of different projects is the same. PI can be calculated as under :-

$$PI = \frac{\text{Present value of Cash inflows}}{\text{Present value of Cash outflows}}$$

If PI>1 the project will be accepted. If PI<1 the project will be rejected. When PI>1,NPV will be positive, when PI<1 NPV will be negative. In case, more than one project have PI>1 then the project whose PI is the highest will be given first preference and the project with minimum PI will be given last preference.

Implementation

Every entrepreneur should draw an implementation scheme or a time table for his project to ensure the timely completion of all activities involved in setting upon enterprise. Timely implementation is important because if there is delay it causes, among other things, a project cost overrun. In India delay in project implementation has become a common feature.

Implementation phase for an industrial project, which involves settings up of manufacturing facilities, consists of several stages. These are :-

- ➢ Project and engineering design
- ➢ Negotiation and contracting
- ➢ Construction
- ➢ Training
- ➢ Plant and commissioning

Translating an investment proposal into a concrete projects is a complex, time consuming and risky task. Delays in implementation, which are common can lead to substantial cost overruns. For expeditious implementation at a reasonable cost, the following are useful :

- ➢ Adequate formulation projects
- ➢ Use of the principle of responsibility accounting
- ➢ Use of network techniques

Hence, there is a need to draw up an implementation schedule for the project and then to adhere. Following is a simplified implementation schedule for a small project

An illustrative implementation schedule

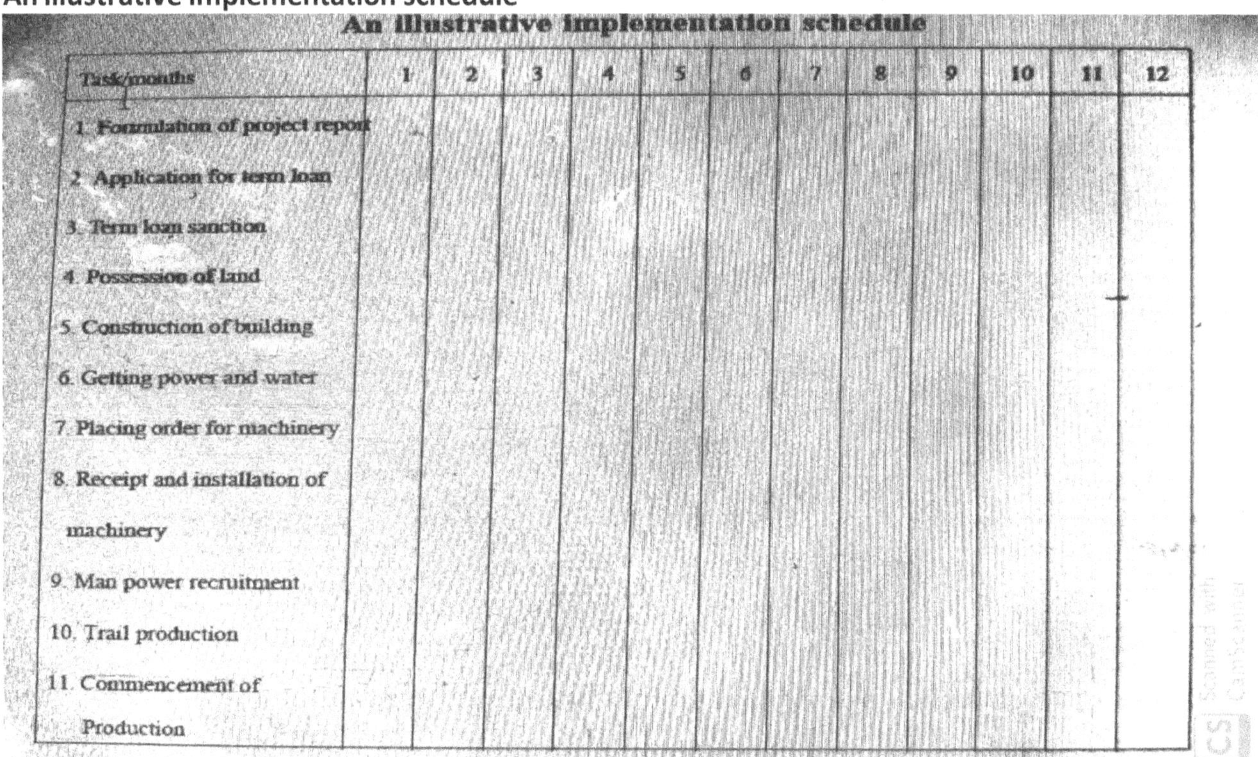

Task/months	1	2	3	4	5	6	7	8	9	10	11	12
1. Formulation of project report												
2. Application for term loan												
3. Term loan sanction												
4. Possession of land												
5. Construction of building												
6. Getting power and water												
7. Placing order for machinery												
8. Receipt and installation of machinery												
9. Man power recruitment												
10. Trail production												
11. Commencement of Production												

The above schedule can be broken up into scores of specific tasks involved in setting up the enterprise. Project evaluation and review technique (PERT) and critical path method (CPM) can also be used to get better in sight into all activities related to implementation of the project.

Review

Once the project is commissioned, the review phase has to be set in motion. Performance review should be dome periodically compare actual performance with projected performance. A feedback device is useful in several ways.

- ➢ It throws light on how realistic were the assumption underlying the project.

- ➢ It provides a documented log of experience that is highly valuable in future decision.
- ➢ It suggests corrective action to be taken in the light of actual performance.
- ➢ It helps in uncovering judgmental basis.

RESOURCE ALLOCATION FRAMEWORK

The resource allocation framework of the firm, which shapes, guides, and circumscribes individual project decisions, addresses two key issues : What should be the strategic posture of the firm ? What pattern of resource allocation sub serves the chosen strategic posture ?. It is divided into following section :

- Key criteria
- Elementary investment strategies
- Portfolio planning tools
- Strategic position and action evaluation

Key criteria

The objective of maximising the wealth of shareholders is reflected, at the operational level, in three key criteria : profitability, risk, and growth.

1. Profitability : Profitability reflects the relationship between profit and investment. While there are numerous ways of measuring profitability, return on equity is one of the most widely used method. It is defined as :

$$\text{Profitability} = \frac{\text{Profit after tax}}{\text{Net Worth}}$$

2. Risk :- It reflects variability. How much do individual outcomes deviate from the expected value ? A simple measure of variability is the range of possible outcomes, which is simply the difference between the highest and net outcomes.

3. Growth :- This is manifested in the increase of revenue, assets, net worth, profits, dividends, and so on. To reflect the growth of a variable, the measure commonly employed is the compound rate of growth.

SENSITIVITY ANALYSIS

Sensitivity analysis is the use of multiple what-if scenarios to model a range of possible outcomes. The technique is used to evaluate alternative business decisions, employing different assumptions about variables. For example, a financial analyst could examine the potential profit levels that may be achieved as a result of an investment in machinery by altering the expected demand level, material costs, equipment downtime percentage, crewing costs, and residual value of the equipment.

For example, an analyst is modeling the range of profit outcomes for a prospective equipment purchase. A potential issue is that the equipment may be superseded by a new equipment model, which may reduce its resale value. Accordingly, the analyst conducts a sensitivity analysis that models the lifetime profitability of the investment, assuming a range of possible resale values at the end of the projected usage period for the equipment.A particularly useful aspect of sensitivity analysis is to locate those variables that can have an unusually large impact on the outcome of the analysis. The decision maker can then evaluate the probability of the variables experiencing significant changes. The outcome is a better understanding of the risks associated with an investment.One way to create a sensitivity analysis is to aggregate variables into three scenarios, which are the worst case, most likely case, and best case. The probability of occurrence for the variables used in these three cases clusters the highest probability variables in the most likely case.

PROJECT FINANCING IN INDIA

 INTRODUCTION

Finance is the lubricant of the process of economic growth. When finance mode is available, industrial activities can be initiated which gives rise to new investment opportunities towards industrialization. The Indian financial institutions have been very important constituent of the Indian economy. This importance they have derived from their financial muscle and they have linked it to the industrial development in the country. For years now the Indian financial institutions have been the life line of credit for the Indian corporate. This has been mainly because of their strong financial muscle and the various concessions they received from the Central Government for their role. In India, special financial institutions have been developed to provide finance to the upliftment of industrial activities in all regions so as to sustain an equitable industrial growth in the county. Financial assistance is being extended to the industrial enterprises by the financial institutions and development banks on confessional terms of finance as per their bye laws in the state.

MEANING AND IMPORTANCE OF PROJECT FINANCE

Project finance refers to the financing of long-term infrastructure, industrial projects and public services based upon a non-recourse or limited recourse financial structure where project debt and equity used to finance the project are paid back from the cash flow generated by the project. Project finance is used by private sector companies as a means of funding major projects off balance sheet. At the heart of the project finance transaction is the concession company, a special purpose Vehicle (SPV) which consists of the consortium shareholders who may be investors or have other interests in the project (such as contractor or operator). The SPV is created as an independent legal entity which enters into contractual agreements with a number of other parties necessary in the project finance deals.The attractiveness of project finance is the ability to fund projected in the off balance sheet with limited or non-recourse to the equity investors i.e. if a project fails, the project lenders recourse is to ownership of the actual project and they are unable to pursue the equity investors for debt. For this reason lenders focus on the projects cash flow as the main source for repaying project debt.

Importance of Project finance

Project financing is being used throughout the world across a wide range of industries and sectors. This funding technique is growing in popularity as governments seek to involve the private sector in the funding and operation of public infrastructure. Private sector investment and management of public sector assets is being openly encouraged by governments and multilateral agencies who recognize that private sector companies are better equipped and more efficient than government in developing and managing major public services. Project finance is used extensively in the following sectors.

- Oil and gas
- Mining
- Electricity Generation
- Water
- Telecommunications
- Road and highways
- Railways and Metro systems
- Public services

MEANS OF FINANCE AND SOURCES OF PROJECT IN INDIA

The long-term sources of finance used for meeting the cost of project are referred to as the means of finance. To meet the cost of project, the following sources of finance may be available

- Equity Capital
- Preference Capital
- Debentures
- Rupees term loans
- Foreign currency term loans
- Euro issues
- Deferred credit
- Bill rediscounting scheme
- Suppliers line of credit
- Seed capital assistance
- Government subsidies
- Sales tax deferment and exemption
- Unsecured loans and deposits
- Lease and hire purchase finance
- Public Deposit
- Bank Credit

Equity Capital

This is the contribution made by the owners of business, the equity shareholders, who enjoy the rewards and bear the risks of ownership. However, their liabilities, limited to their capital contribution. From the point of view of the issuing film, equity capital offers, two important advantages: (i) It represents permanent capital. Hence there is no liability for repayment. (ii) It does not involve any fixed obligation for payment of dividend. The disadvantages of raising funds by way of equity capital are : (i) The cost of equity capital is high because equity dividend are not tax-deductible expenses. (ii) The cost of issuing equity capital is high.

Preference Capital

A hybrid form of financing, preference capital partakes some characteristics of equity capital and some attributes of debt capital. It is similar, to equity capital because preference dividend, like equity dividend, is not a tax-deductible payment. It resembles debt capital because the rate of preference dividend is fixed. Typically, when preference dividend is skipped it is payable in future because of the cumulative feature associated with it. The near-fixity of preference dividend payment renders preference capital somewhat unattractive in general as a source of finance. It is, however, attractive when the promoters do not want a reduction in their share: share of equity and yet there is need for widening the net worth base (net worth consists of equity and preference capital) to satisfy the requirements of financial institutions. In addition to the conventional preference shares, a company may issue Cumulative Convertible Preference Shares (CCPS). These shares carry a dividend rate of 10 per cent (which; if unpaid, cumulates) and are compulsory convertible into equity shares between three and five years from the date of issue.

Debenture Capital

In the last few years, debenture capital has emerged as an important source for project financing. There are three types of debentures that are commonly used in India: Non-Convertible Debentures (NCDs), Partially Convertible Debentures (PCDs), and Fully Convertible Debentures (FCDs). Akin to promissory, NCDs are used by companies for raising debt that is generally retired over a period of 5 to 10 years. They are secured by a charge on the assets of the issuing company. PCDs are partly convertible into equity shares as per pre-determined terms of conversion. The unconverted portion of PCDs remains like NCDs. FCDs, as the name implies, are converted wholly into equity shares as per pre-determined terms of conversion. Hence FCDs may be regarded as delayed equity instruments.

Rupee Term Loans

Provided by financial institutions and commercial banks, rupee term loans which represent secured borrowings are a very important source for financing new projects as well as expansion, modernisation, and renovation schemes of existing units. These loans are generally repayable over a period of 8-10 years which includes a moratorium period of I-3 years.

Foreign Currency Terms Loans

Financial institutions provide foreign currency term loans for-meeting the foreign currency expenditures towards import of plant, machinery, equipment and also towards payment of foreign technical know-how fees. Under the general scheme, the periodical liability towards interest and principal remains in the currency/currencies of the loan/s and is translated into rupees at the then prevailing rate of exchange for making payments to the financial institution. Apart from approaching financial institutions (which typically serve as intermediaries between foreign agencies and Indian borrowers), companies can directly obtain foreign currency loans from international lenders. More and more companies appear to be doing so presently.

Euro issues

Beginning with Reliance Industries' Global Depository Receipts issue of approximately $150 ml in May 1992, a number of companies have been making euro issues. They have employed two types of securities: Global Depository Receipts (GDRs) and Euroconvertible Bonds (ECBs). . Denominated in US dollars, a GDR is a negotiable certificate that represents the publicly traded local currency (Indian Rupee) equity shares of a non-US (Indian) company. (Of course, in. theory, a GDR may represent a debt security; in practice it rarely does so.) GDRs are issued by the Depository Bank (such as the Bank of New York) against the local currency shares (such as Rupee shares) which are delivered to the depository's local custodian banks. GDRs trade freely in the overseas markets. A Euroconvertible Bond (ECB) is an equity-linked debt security. The holder of an ECB has the option to convert it into equity shares at a pre-determined conversion ratio during a specified period. ECBs are regarded as advantageous by the issuing company because (i) they carry a lower rate of interest compared to a straight debt security, (ii) they do not lead to dilution of earnings per share in the near future, and (iii) they carry very few restrictive covenants.

Deferred Credit

Many a time the suppliers of machinery provide deferred credit facility under which payment for the purchase of machinery is made over a period of time. The interest rate on deferred credit and the period of payment vary rather widely. Normally, the supplier of machinery when he offers deferred credit facility insists that the bank guarantee should be furnished by the buyer.

Bills Rediscounting Scheme

Operated by the IDBI, the bills rediscounting scheme is meant to promote the sale of indigenous machinery on deferred payment basis. Under this scheme, the seller realizes the sale proceeds by discounting the bills or promissory notes accepted by the buyer with a commercial bank which in turn rediscounts them with the IDBI. This scheme is meant primarily for balancing equipments and machinery required for expansion, modernisation, and replacement schemes.

Suppliers' Line of Credit

Administered by the ICICI, the Suppliers' Line of Credit is somewhat similar to the IDBI's Bill Rediscounting Scheme. Under this arrangement, ICICI directly pays to the machinery manufacturer against usance bills duly accepted or guaranteed by the bank of the purchaser.

Seed Capital Assistance

Financial institutions, through what may be labelled broadly as the 'Seed Capital Assistance scheme, seek to supplement the resources of the promoters and of medium scale industrial units which are eligible for assistance from All-India financial institutions and/ or state-level financial institutions. Broadly three schemes have been formulated:

(i) *Special Seed Capital Assistance Scheme* The quantum of assistance under this scheme is Rs 0.2 million or 20 per cent of the project cost, whichever is lower. This scheme is administered by the State. Financial Corporations.

(ii) *Seed Capital Assistance Scheme* The assistance order this scheme is applicable to projects costing not more then Rs 20 million. The assistance per project is restricted to Rs 1.5 million. The assistance is provided by IDBI through state level financial institutions. In special cases, the IDBI may provide the assistance directly.

(iii) *Risk Capital Foundation Scheme* Under this scheme, the Risk Capital Foundation, an autonomous foundation set up and funded by the IFCI, offers assistance to promoters of projects costing between Rs 20 million and Rs 150 million. The ceiling on the assistance provided between Rs 1.5 million and Rs 4 million depending on the number of applicant promoters.

Government Subsidies

Previously the central government as well as the state governments provided subsidies to industrial units located in backward areas. The central subsidy has been discontinued but the state subsidies continue. The state subsidies vary between 5 per cent to 25 per cent of the fixed capital investment in the project, subject to a ceiling varying between Rs 0.5 million and Rs 2.5 million depending on the location.

Sales Tax. Deferments and Exemptions

To attract industries, the states provide incentives, *inter alia,* in the form of sales tax deferments and sales tax exemptions. Under the sales tax deferment scheme, the payment of sales tax on the sale of finished goods may be deferred for a period ranging between five to twelve years. Essentially, it implies that the project gets an interest free loan, represented by the quantum of sales tax deferred, during the deferent period. Under the sales tax exemption scheme, some states exempt the payment of sales tax applicable on purchases of raw materials, consumables, packing, and processingmaterials from within the state which are used for manufacturing purposes. The period of exemption ranges from three to nine years depending upon the state and the specific location of the project within the state.

Unsecured Loans and Deposits

Unsecured loans are typically provided by the promoters to fill the gap between the promoters' contribution required by financial institutions and the equity capital subscribed by the promoters. These loans are subsidiary to the institutional loans. The rate of interest chargeable on these loans is less than the rate of interest on the institutional loans. Finally these loans cannot be taken back without the prior approval of financial institutions.Deposits from public, referred to as public deposits, represent unsecured borrowing of two to three years' duration. Many existing companies prefer to raise public deposits instead of term loans from financial institutions because restrictive covenants do not accompany public deposits. However, it may not be possible for a new company to raise public deposits. Further, it maybe difficult for it to repay public deposits within three years.

Foreign Currency Loans

Apart from rupee term loans, financial institutions provide foreign currency loans. This assistance is now provided only for the import of capital equipment (as per the liberalised exchange risk management system, foreign currency required for other purposes has to be purchased from authorised dealers at market rates). On foreign currency loans sanctioned under the general scheme, the interest rate charged is typically a floating rate as determined by the lenders, (the foreign agency that has given a line of credit to the financial institution for onward lending) and the risk of exchange rate fluctuation is born by the borrower. On foreign currency loans sanctioned under the Exchange Risk Administration Scheme, the principal repayment obligations of the borrower are rupee tied at the rate of exchange prevailing on the dates of disbursement. On such rupee-tied loan liability, the borrower pays by way of servicing his loan a composite, cost every quarter. The composite cost consists of three elements: (i) the interest portion which is arrived on the basis of the weighted average interest cost of the various components of the currency pool, (ii) the spread of the financial institutions, and (iii) the exchange risk premium. The 'composite cost' is a variable rate determined at six-monthly intervals. It has a floor and a cap. Both the floor and the cap as well as the rate of interest applicable for the period is reviewed and announced from time to time.

Leasing and Hire Purchase Finance

With the emergence of scores of finance companies engaged in the business of leasing and hire purchase finance, it may be possible to get a portion, albeit a small portion, of the assets financed under a lease or a hire purchase arrangement. Typically, a project is financed partly by financial institutions and partly through the resources raised from the capital market. Hence, in finalizing the financing scheme for a project, you should bear in mind the norms and policies of financial institutions and the guidelines of Securities Exchange Board of India and the requirements of the Securities Contracts Regulation Act (SCRA).

Public Deposit

Public deposits have been a peculiar feature or industrial finance in India. Companies have been receiving public deposits for a long time in order to meet their medium-term and long-term requirements for finance. This system was very popular in the cotton textile mills or Bombay, Ahmedabad and Sholapur and in the tea gardens or Assam and Bengal. In recent years, the method or raising finance through the public deposits has again become popular for various reasons. Rates or interest offered by the companies are higher than those offered by banks. At the same time the cost of deposits to the company is less than the cost or borrowings from banks. While accepting public deposits, a company must follow the provisions or the companies Act and the directions issued by the Reserve bank of India. According to the companies (Acceptance of Deposits Rules, 1975 as amended in 1984) Act, no company can receive secure and unsecured deposits in excess of 10% and 25% respectively of paid up share capital plus free reserves. The Central Government has laid down that no company shall invite a deposit unless an advertisement, including a statement showing the financial position of the company, has been issued in the prescribed form. Under the new rule, deposits can be renewed. The rate of interest payable on deposits must not exceed 15% per annum. In order to repay the deposits maturing in a particular year, the company must deposit 110% or the deposits with a scheduled bank or in specified securities.

Bank Credit

Commercial banks in the country serve as the single largest source or short term finance to business firms. They provide it in the form of Outright Loans. Cash credit, and Lines of Credit.

FINANCIAL INSTITUTION STRUCTURE AND FINANCIAL ASSISTANCE

This part concerned with the various aspects of financial institutions and their functioning in India, is divided into six sections as follows :

- Institutional Structure
- Financial assistance : direct and indirect
- Special schemes
- Term loan procedures
- Project appraisal
- Key financial indicators

Institutional Structure

The structure of financial institutions in India is as follows :

I. All India institutions

- Industrial Finance Corporation of India
- Industrial Credit and Investment Corporation of India
- Industrial Development Bank of India
- Other all-India institutions

II. State-level institutions

- State Financial Corporations
- State Industrial Development Corporations

Industrial Finance Corporation of India (IFCI)

Industrial Finance Corporation of India (IFCI)- The IFCI is the first industrial financing institution to be Set up in India soon alter independence. It was set up as a statutory corporation in July, 1948 But was later converted in to a Government Company. The IFCI provides financial assistance to any public limited company and co-operative society registered in India. Such units must be engaged in the manufacture, preservation or processing of goods, or in the shipping, mining or hotel industry, or in the generation and distribution of electricity or any other form of power. Public limited companies in the public sector are also eligible to receive assistance from the IFCI. But proprietary concerns, partnership firms and private companies are not eligible for financial assistance from the corporation. The corporation may grant assistance ranging from Rs.30 lakhs to Rs.2 crores to a single enterprise. Assistance may be given in anyone or more of the above forms for a maximum period of 25 years.

State Financial Corporations (SFC's)- As the Industrial finance Corporation does not provide industrial finance to all types or enterprises, the need was felt for state level financial institutions to finance the needs or non-corporate and other small enterprises. On September 2, 1951, the Parliament passed the State Financial Corporations Act. The Act came in to force with effect from 1st August, 1952. It empowers the State Governments to establish financial institutions for their respective States.

Industrial Credit and Investment Corporation of India (ICICI)

In view of the limited risk capital which IFCI and SFC s provide, need was felt far a more enterprising and flexible institution to facilitate industrial development in the private sector in India. A World Bank-cum-American Investment Mission visited India in 1954 and recommended the establishment or special institution the purpose of assisting industries in the private sector. Accordingly, the ICICI was set up on January 5, 1955 as a public limited company under the Companies Act. The Corporation was set up as a privately owned institution but later on the Life Insurance Corporation of India (a statutory corporation) became its major shareholder. The ICICI has wide powers. It can provide any amount of financial assistance to any public or private company in the private sector. It can now give assistance to projects in the joint sector and co-operative sector. 11 is authorized to provide foreign currency loans to partnerships and proprietary concerns also. Ordinarily Rs.5 lakhs is the minimum limit and Rs.l crore is the higher limit for financial assistance to a single concern. Loans are given generally for the purpose of buying capital assets like land, buildings and machinery. In fact, the ICICI specializes in providing loans in foreign currency. The Corporation helps in the promotion of new enterprises as well as in the expansion and modernization of existing concerns so as to build up a sound industrial.

Industrial Development Bank of India

The Industrial Development Bank of India was established in 1964 as a subsidiary of the Reserve Bank of India. It is headquartered in Bombay. It is the apex term-lending financial institution in India. It has been designated as the principal financial institution of the country for coordinating, in conformity with national priorities, the working of institutions engaged in financing, promoting, and developing industry. IDBI finances the industry directly and also provides principal support to State Finance Corporations and State Industrial Development Corporations and commercial banks in their financing of industries, through refinancing and bill discounting facilities. The resources of IDBI consist of paid-up capital, reserves repayment of loans, market borrowings both within and outside the country, temporary credit from the Reserve Bank of India, and foreign lines of credit from the World Bank, Asian Development Bank and others.

Life Insurance Corporation of India

The Life Insurance Corporation of India (LIC, hereafter) came into being in 1956 after the nationalization and merger of about 250 independent life insurance societies. It is headquartered in Bombay. The primary activity of LIC is to conduct the life insurance business, but it has gradually developed into an important all-India financial institution which provides substantial support to industry.

General Insurance Corporation

The General Insurance Corporation (GIC, hereafter) was founded when the management of general insurance business in India was taken over by the government in 1971 and subsequently nationalised in 1973. It is headquartered in Bombay. GIC provides substantial assistance to industrial projects be way of term loans, subscription to equity capital and debentures, and underwriting of securities.

Industrial Reconstruction Bank of India

The industrial Reconstruction Bank of India, headquartered in Calcutta, was set up when its precursor, the Industrial Reconstruction Corporation of India, was reconstituted in 1984. IRBI is primarily an agency to help the reconstruction and rehabilitation of industrial units which have closed down or which face the risk of closure. IRBI offers assistance in various forms : (i) financial assistance which is not available from normal channels of finance and banking, (ii) technical assistance and guidance to sick units to revive them, (iii) managerial in the fields of administration, finance, marketing, industrial relations, etc. and (iv) suggestions for reconstruction and rationalization.

State   Level   Institutions

State Financial Corporations

The State Financial Corporation, set up under the State Financial Corporation Act, 1951, render assistance to medium and small scale industries in their respective states. Their shareholders are the respective state governments, IDBI, insurance companies, credit cooperatives and private shareholders.

State Industrial and Development Corporations

The State Industrial Development Corporation, were set up by the state governments during the 1960s to serve as catalytic agents in the industrialization process of their respective states. Presently almost every state has an SIDC which is fully owned by the respective state government.

Financial Assistance : Direct and Indirect

Direct Financial Assistance

Financial institutions provide direct financial assistance in the following ways :

• Rupee term loans
• Foreign currency term loans
• Subscription to equity shares
• Seed capital

Indirect Financial Assistance

Besides providing direct financial assistance, financial institutions extend help to industrial units in obtaining finance/credit through the following ways :

- Deferred payment guarantee
- Guarantee for foreign currency loans
- Underwriting

Deferred Payment Guarantee

Financial institutions issue guarantee on behalf of the buyer of industrial machinery to the supplier offering the facility of deferred payments. Should there be a default by the buyer in the payment of deferred installments, financial institutions make the payment and subsequently recover the amount form the assisted unit. A nominal commission is charged for providing such guarantee.

Guarantee for Foreign Currency Loans

Financial institutions provide guarantee for foreign currency loans obtained by industrial concerns from institutions and banks abroad. A nominal commission is charged to the assisted unit for such guarantee.

Underwriting

As part of the overall financial package, financial institutions generally participate in underwriting equity issues of assisted units. This helps the assisted units in raising funds from the capital market.

Special Schemes

Several special schemes have been designed to serve the varied needs of industry. The important ones are :

- Bill rediscounting scheme
- Suppliers line of credit
- Soft loan scheme
- Equipment finance scheme

NORMS OF FINANCE AND TERM LOAN PROCEDURE

The principal norms and policies of financial institutions are described below:

Eligibility

Till recently, long term loans were provided by financial institutions to concerns in certain industries and denied to concerns in industries placed in the negative list.mNow, however, a shift is taking place in their policy, They are inclined to finance almost every kind of industry. Further, till recently financial institutions followed a consortium approach as per the advice of the Ministry of Finance. Now they are permitted to lend individually as well as participate in consortium lending.

Debt-equity Ratio

Presently, the general debt-equity norm for medium and large scale projects is 1.5:1. This serves as a broad guideline against which variations are permitted on a case to case basis, especially under the following circumstances: (a) high degree of capital intensity, (b) location in a backward area, and (c) background' of the promoter. Other things being equal: (i) a capital intensive project is eligible for a higher debt-equity ratio, (ii) a project in a backward area qualifies for a higher debt-equity ratio, and (ill) a project promoted by a technocrat-promoter is entitled to a higher debt-equity ratio. How are debt and equity defined for the purpose of calculating the debt-equity ratio? Debt consists of the following: (i) loans and deposits that are repayable after one year (this includes interest bearing unsecured loans from government agencies, promoters, etc.), (ii) non-convertible debentures and convertible debentures (except that part which is compulsorily convertible into equity) until they are converted, irrespective of the maturity period, (ill) deferred payments, and (iv) preference shares due for redemption within three years. Equity consists of the following: (i) paid-up ordinary share capital, (ii) irredeemable preference shares, cumulative convertible preference shares where the redemption period is due after three years, (iii) premium on share issues, (iv) central/ state cash subsidy, (v) long term interest-free unsecured loans from state governments or government agencies or promoters subordinate to loan from financial institutions, and (vi) free reserves (including surplus in profit and loss account) less any accumulated losses, arrears or unabsorbed depreciation, intangible assets (like goodwill), expenditures not written off (like preliminary expenses), and investments in other undertakings where these are 'prima facie' considered unrealisable.

Promoters Contribution

Financial institutions require promoters to contribute 25 to 30 per cent of the project cost. This is lowered selectively in certain cases like capital-intensive projects, high priority projects, and technocrat-promoted projects. Contributions made by the following or of the following kinds represent promoters' contribution (i) equity investment by promoters, their friends, relatives and associates (including NRIs), (ii) equity investment by other companies controlled by promoters, (iii) equity participation by shareholders of other promoter companies, (iv) foreign collaborators,' (v) investment from oil exporting developing countries, (vi) state government, in the case of joint sector or assisted sector projects, (vii) seed capital assistance, (viii) unsecured loan from promoters, (ix) venture capital participation, (x) mutual fund participation, (xi) internal accruals in the case of an existing company, (xii) rights issue to existing shareholders, and (xiii) any other contribution approved as promoters' contribution.

Term Loan Procedure

The procedure associated with a term loan involves the following principal steps.

1. Submission of loan application
   The borrower may submit the application to any of the three term lending institutions, viz, IDBI, ICICI, and IFCI. The borrower is required to fill out a common application form.
2. Initial processing of loan application
3. Appraisal of the proposed projects
4. Issue of the letter of sanction
5. Acceptance of the terms and conditions by the borrowing unit
6. Execution of loan agreement
7. Disbursement of loans
8. Creation of security
9. Monitoring

FINANCIAL ANALYSIS

Financial analysis is defined as the process of discovering economic facts about an enterprise and/or a project on the basis of an interpretation of financial data. Financial analysis also seeks to look at the capital cost, operations cost and operating revenue. The analysis decisively establishes a relationship between the various factors of a project and helps in maneuvering the project's activities. It also serves as a common measure of value for obtaining a clear-cut understanding about the project from the financial point of view. An analysis of several financial tools provide an important basis for valuing securities and appraising managerial programmes. Financial analysis is vital in the interpretation of financial statements. It can provide an insight into two important areas of management— return on investment and soundness of the company's financial position.Internal management accounts provide information which is valuable for the purpose of control. The information is made available in the form of accounting data, which may be manifested as financial and accounting statements. A financial analysis reveals where the company stands with respect to profitability, liquidity, leverage and an efficient use of its assets. Financial reports provide the framework within which business planning takes place. They are the key through which an effective control of a business enterprise is exercised. It is the process of determining the significant financial characteristics of a firm. It may be external or internal. The external analysis is performed by creditors, stockholders and investment analysis. The internal analysis is performed by various departments of a firm.

Significance of financial analysis

Financial analysis primarily deals with the interpretation of the data incorporated in the proforma financial statements of a project and the presentation of the data in a form in which it can be utilized for a comparative appraisal of the projects. It is, in effect, concerned with the development of the financial profile of the project. Its purpose is to find out whether the project is attractive enough to secure funds needed for its various constituent activities and once having secured the funds,whether the project will be able to generate enough economic values to achieve the objectives for which it is sought to be implemented. It deals not only with the financial aspects of a project but also with its operational aspects. As such, it is necessary to undertake such an analysis not only in the case of industrial projects but also in the case of non-industrial projects. Analysis of financial statements has become very significant due to the widespread interest of various parties in the financial results of a company. In recent years, the ownership of capital of most public companies has become broad-based. A number of parties and bodies, including creditors, potential suppliers, debenture-holders, credit institutions like banks, industrial finance corporations, potential investors, employees, trade unions, important customers, economists, investment analysts, taxation authorities and government have a stake in the financial results of a company. Various people look at the financial statements from various angles. A number of techniques have been developed to undertake analysis of financial statements in order to reach conclusions about the financial health, profitability and efficiency of an enterprise and also to compare an enterprise with other similar undertakings. The technique of ratio analysis is the most important tool of financial analysis. It helps in comparing the performance of various companies and judge their financial soundness.

Utility of financial and accounting statements

Financial statements play a vital role in the internal financial control of an enterprise. These should, therefore, the properly constructed,analyzed and interpreted by executives, bankers, creditors and investors. The entire future of a company hinges on the manager's ability to decide relevant financial data with a view to planning profit ability moves. Learning to read financial statements is the first essential element in any businessman's attempt to acquire financial management skills. The change in the elitism of stock ownership to broad public ownership has necessitated a concomitant change in the entire process of reporting corporate financial results. The role of management in the matter of preparation of financial statements is to add understanding to these statements, the fairness of which is to be viewed through the eye of the user, while that of the accountant is to close the communication gap and of the auditor to add credibility to them. For evolving a good economic information system, accounting innovations are of great economic information system. Without these, communication with the financial community would be difficult, the interest of present and future potential investors would not be served, the ability of the company to raise additional capital would be impaired and the government's regulatory measures and policies would not serve the best interest of society. Though a financial statement reveals less than it conceals, it provides the indicators of the enterprise's performance during the year. Financial analysis seeks to spotlight the significant facts and relationships concerning managerial performance, viz., corporate efficiency, financial strengths and weaknesses and creditworthiness of the enterprise.

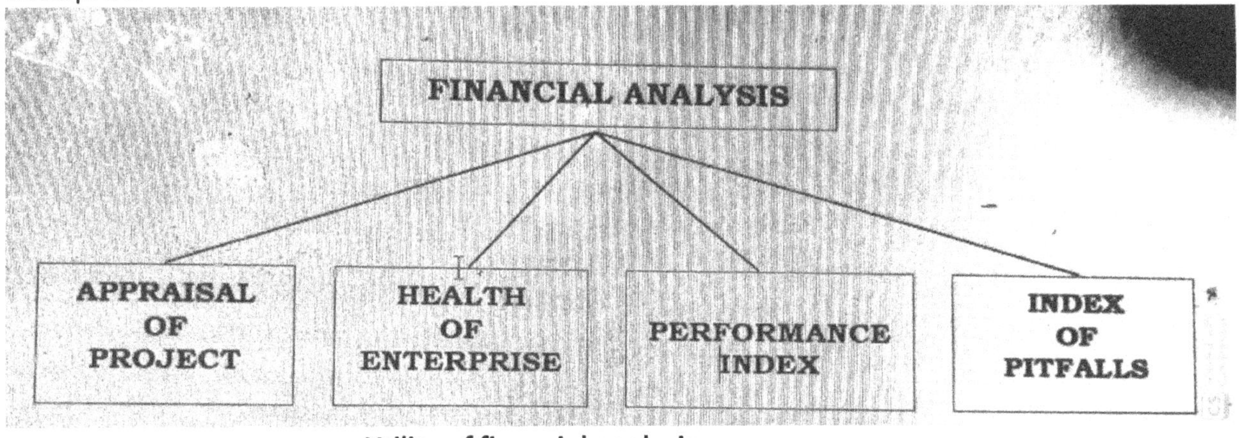

. Utility of financial analysis

SOCIAL COST-BENEFIT ANALYSIS
INTRODUCTION

The term "social costs" refers to all those harmful consequences and damages which the community on the whole sustains as a result of productive processes and for which private entrepreneurs are not held responsible. The definition of the concept is comprehensive enough to include even certain "social opportunity costs", avoidable wastes and social inefficiencies of various kinds. Implicit in such an appraisal is the assumption that the principal objective of investment decision-making is to maximize the net present value of monetary flow or some variant of it. The social cost-benefit analysis is a tool for evaluating the value of money, particularly of public investments in many economies. It aids in making decisions with respect to the various aspects of a project and the design programs of closely interrelated projects. Cost benefit analysis has become important among economists and consultants in recent years.

NEED FOR COST-BENEFIT ANALYSIS

The essence of the theory of social cost-benefit analysis is that it does not accept that the actual receipts of a project adequately measure social benefits and actual expenditures measure social costs. The reason is that actual prices may be an inadequate indicator of economic benefits and costs. For example, in developing countries like India, the prices of necessities are set low, despite their economic importance, while the prices of less essential goods are set high (through a system of taxes and duties). As a result, some projects which appear very profitable when their outputs and inputs are valued at actual prices are, in fact, unattractive from the viewpoint of the national economy, while other apparently unprofitable projects have high economic returns. But the theory accepts that actual receipts and expenditures can be suitably adjusted so that the difference between them, closely analogous to ordinary profit, will properly reflect the social gain. In Social-Cost Benefit Analysis (SCBA) the focus is on social costs and benefits of a project. These often tend to differ from the costs incurred in monetary terms and benefits earned in monetary terms by the project.

The principal reasons for discrepancy are:

(i) *Market imperfections:* Market prices, which form the basis for computing the monetary costs and benefits from the point of view of project sponsor, reflect social values only under conditions of perfect competition, which are rarely, if ever, realized by developing countries. When imperfections obtain, market prices do not reflect social values. The common market imperfections found in developing countries are: (i) rationing, (ii) prescription of minimum wage rates, and (iii) foreign exchange regulation. Rationing of a commodity means control over its price and distribution. The price paid by a consumer under rationing is often significantly less than the price that would prevail in a competitive market. When minimum wage rates are prescribed, the wages paid to labour are usually more than what the wages would be in a competitive labour market free from such wage legislations. The official rate of foreign exchange in most of the developing countries, which exercise close regulation over foreign exchange, is typically less than the rate that would prevail in the absence of foreign exchange regulation. This is why foreign exchange usually commands premium in unofficial transactions.

(ii) *Externalities*: A project may have beneficial external effects. For example, it may create certain infrastructural facilities like roads which benefit the neighbouring areas. Such benefits are considered in SCBA, though they are ignored in assessing the monetary benefits to the project sponsors because they do not receive any monetary compensation from those who enjoy this external benefit created by the project. Likewise, a project may have a harmful external effect like environmental pollution. In SCBA, the cost of such environmental pollution is relevant, though the project sponsors do not incur any monetary costs. It may be emphasized that externalities are relevant in SCBA because in such analysis all costs and benefits, irrespective to whom they accrue and whether they are paid for or not, are relevant.

(iii) *Taxes and subsidies*: From the private point of view, taxes are definite monetary costs and subsidies are definite monetary gains. From the social point of view, however, taxes and subsidies are generally regarded as transfer payments and hence considered irrelevant.

(iv) *Concern for savings*: Unconcerned about how its benefits are divided between consumption and savings, a private firm does not put differential valuation on savings and consumption. From a social point of view, however, the division of benefits between consumption and savings (which leads to investment) is relevant particularly in capital-scarce developing countries. A rupee of benefits saved is deemed more valuable than a rupee of benefits consumed. The concern of society for savings and investment is duly reflected in SCBA wherein a higher valuation is placed on savings and lower valuation is put on consumption.

(v) *Concern for redistribution*: A private firm does not bother how its benefits are distributed across various groups in the society. The society, however, is concerned about the distribution of benefits across different groups. A rupee of benefit going to a poor section is considered more valuable than a rupee of benefit going to an affluent section.

(vi) *Merit wants*: Goals and preferences not expressed in the market place, but believed by policy makers to be in the larger social interest, may be referred to as merit wants. For example, the government may prefer to promote adult education or a balanced nutrition programme for school-going children even though these are not sought by consumers in the market place. While merit wants are not relevant from the private point of view, they are important from the social point of view.

PROCEDURE OF SCBA

The objective of social cost-benefit analysis is, in its widest sense, to secure and achieve the value of money in economic life by simply evaluating the costs and benefits of alternative economic choices and selecting an alternative which offers the largest net benefit, i.e. the highest margin of benefit over cost. Very broadly, social-cost benefit analysis involves the following steps:

1. Estimates of costs and benefits which will accrue to the project implementing body.
2. Estimates of costs and benefits which will accrue to individual members of society as consumers or as suppliers of factor input.
3. Estimates of costs and benefits which will accrue to the community.
4. Estimates of costs and benefits which will accrue to the National Exchequer.
5. Discounting the costs and benefits which accrue over a period of time to determine the feasibility of the project. Here again, the non-quantifiable benefits are stated only in descriptive terms. These strategies will work towards the appropriate calculation of the profitability ratio. While this is the general approach to project formulation, implementation and evaluation, the same may be modified to suit the circumstances.

MAIN FEATURES OF SOCIAL COST-BENEFIT ANALYSIS

Prest and Turvey defined cost-benefit analysis as "a practical way of assessing the desirability of projects, where it is important to take a long view in the sense (looking at repercussions in the future as well as the near future and a wide view in the sense of allowing side-effects of many decisions relating to industries, regions etc.), i.e., it implies the enumeration and evaluation of all the relevant cost and benefits". This definition focuses attention on the main features of cost-benefit analysis.

It covers five distinct issues:

1. Assessing the desirability of projects in the public, as opposed to the private sector.
2. Identification of costs and benefits.
3. Measurement of costs and benefits.
4. The effect of (risk and uncertainty) time in investment appraisal.
5. Presentation of results– the investment criterion.

UNITED NATIONS INDUSTRIAL DEVELOPMENT ORGANISATION (UNIDO) APPROACH

Towards the end of the sixties and in the early seventies two principal approaches for SCBA emerged: the UNIDO approach and the Little- Mirrlees approach. This section discusses the UNIDO approach; the following discusses the Little-Mirrlees approach.

The UNIDO method of project appraisal involves five stages:

1. Calculation of financial profitability of the project measured at market prices.
2. Obtaining the net benefit of project measured in terms of economic (efficiency) prices.
3. Adjustment for the impact of the project on savings and investment.
4. Adjustment for the impact of the project on income distribution.

5. Adjustment for the impact of project on merit goods and demerit goods whose social values differ from their economic values.

Each stage of appraisal measures the desirability of the project from a different angle. The measurement of financial profitability of the project in the first stage is similar to the financial evaluation. So, skipping the first stage, the remaining stages are being discussed here.

Net benefit in terms of economic (efficiency) prices

Stage two of the UNIDO approach is concerned with the determination of the net benefit of the project in terms of economic (efficiency) prices, also referred to as shadow prices. The UNIDO approach suggests three sources of shadow pricing, depending on the impact of the project on national economy. A project as it uses and produces resources may for any given input or output (i) increase or decrease the total consumption in the economy, (ii) decrease or increase production in the economy, (iii) decrease imports or increase imports, or (iv) increase exports or decrease exports. If the impact of the project is on consumption in the economy the basis of shadow pricing is consumer willingness to pay. If the impact of the project is on production in the economy, the basis of shadow pricing is the cost of production. If the impact of project is on international trade increase in exports, decrease in imports, increase in imports, or decrease in exports— the basis of shadow pricing is the foreign exchange value.

Shadow pricing of tradable inputs and outputs: A good is fully traded when an increase in its consumption results in a corresponding increase in import or decrease in export or when an increase in its production results in a corresponding increase in export or decrease in import. For fully traded goods, the shadow price is the border price, translated in domestic currency at market exchange rate. The above definition of a fully traded good implies that domestic changes in demand or supply affect just the level of imports or exports.

Non-tradable inputs and outputs: A good is non-tradable when the following conditions are satisfied: I) its import price (CIF price) is greater than its domestic cost of production and (ii) its export price (FOB price) is less than its domestic cost of production. The valuation of non-tradables is done as per the principles of shadow pricing discussed earlier. On the output side, if the impact of the project is to increase the consumption of the product in the economy, the measure of value is the marginal consumers' willingness to pay; if the impact of the project is to substitute other production of the same non tradable in the economy, the measure of value is the saving in cost of production. On the input side, if the impact of the project is to reduce the availability of the input to other users, their willingness to pay for the input represents social value; if the project's input requirement is met by additional production of it, the production cost of it is the measure of social value.

Externalities: An externality, also referred to as an external effect, is a special class of good which has the following characteristics: (i) It is not deliberately created by the project sponsor but is an incidental outcome of legitimate economic activity, (ii) It is beyond the control of the persons who are affected by it, for better or for worse. (iii) It is not traded in the market place. An external effect may be beneficial or harmful. Examples of beneficial external effects are:

(i) An oil company drilling in its own fields may generate useful information about oil potential in the neighbouring fields.

(ii) The approach roads built by a company may improve the transport system in that area.

(iii) The training programme of a firm may upgrade the skills of its workers thereby enhancing their earning power in subsequent employments.

Examples of harmful external effects are:

(i) A factory may cause environmental pollution by emitting large volume of smoke and dirt. People living in the neigbourhood may be exposed to health hazards and put to inconvenience.

(ii) The location of an airport in a certain area may raise noise levels considerably in the neighbourhood.

(iii) A highway may cut a farmer's holding in two, separating his grazing land and his cowsheds, thereby adversely affecting his physical output. Since SCBA seeks to consider all costs and benefits, to whomsoever they may affect, external effects need to be taken into account. The valuation of external effects is rather difficult because they are often intangible in nature and there is no market price, which can be used as a starting point. Their values are estimated by indirect means. The above examples serve to emphasize the difficulties in measuring external effects. In view of this, some economists have suggested that these effects be ignored. In order to justify their suggestion, they argue that since a project is likely to have both beneficial and harmful external effects, one may not err much in assuming that the net effect would be zero. This argument, seemingly a rationalization for one's ignorance, lacks validity. External effects must be taken into account wherever it is possible to do so. Even if these effects cannot be measured in monetary terms, some qualitative evaluation must be attempted.

Measurement of the impact on distribution

Stages three and four of the UNIDO method are concerned with measuring the value of a project in terms of its contribution to savings and income redistribution. To facilitate such assessments we must first measure the income gained or lost by individual groups within the society.

For income distribution analysis, the society may be divided into various groups. The UNIDO approach seeks to identify income gains and losses by the following: (i) Project, (ii) Other private business, (iii) Government, (iv) Workers, (v) Consumers, (vi) External sector. There are, however, other equally valid groupings. The gain or loss to an individual group within the society as a result of the project is equal to the difference between shadow price and market price of each input or output in the case of physical resources or the difference between price paid and value received in the case of financial transaction.

Savings impact and its value— Most of the developing countries face scarcity of capital. Hence the governments of these countries are concerned about the impact of a project on savings and its value thereof. Stage three of the UNIDO method, concerned with this, seeks to answer the following questions:

(i) Given the income distribution impact of the project what would be its effect on savings?

(ii) What is the value of such savings to the society?

Impact on savings of a project is equal to

$$\Sigma \Delta Y_i MPS_i$$

where, ΔY_i = change in income of group i as a result of the project

MPS_i = marginal propensity to save of group i

Value of savings of a rupee is the present value of the additional consumption stream produced when that rupee of savings is invested at the margin. The additional stream of consumption generated by a rupee of investment depends on the marginal productivity of capital and the rate of reinvestment from additional income. If the marginal productivity of capital is r and the rate of reinvestment from additional income a, the additional stream of consumption generated by a rupee of investment can be worked out. The consumption stream starts with r (1 – a) and grows annually at the rate of ar forever. Its present value when discounted at the social discount rate k is:

$$I = \frac{r(1-a)}{(1+k)} + \frac{r(1-a)(1+ar)}{(1+k)^2} + \cdots + \frac{r(1-a)(1+ar)^{n-1}}{(1+k)^n} + \cdots$$

$$= \frac{\dfrac{r(1-a)}{(1+k)}}{1 - \dfrac{(1+ar)}{(1+k)}} = \frac{r(1-a)}{(k-ar)}$$

where, I = social value of a rupee of savings (investment)

r = marginal productivity of capital

a = reinvestment rate on additional income arising from investment

k = social discount rate.

Income distribution impact— Many governments regard redistribution of income in favour of economically weaker sections or economically backward regions as a socially desirable objective. Due to practical difficulties in pursuing the objective of redistribution entirely through the tax, subsidy, and transfer measures of the government, investment projects are also considered as instruments for income redistribution and their contribution toward this goal is considered in their evaluation. This calls for suitably weighing the net gain or loss by each groups, measured earlier, to reflect the relative value of income for different groups and summing them.

Adjustment for merit and demerit goods

In some case, the analysis has to be extended beyond stage four to reflect the difference between the economic value and social value of resources. This difference exists in the case of merit goods and demerit goods. A merit good is one for which the social value exceeds the economic value. For example, a country may place a higher social value than economic value on production of oil because it reduces dependence on foreign supplies. The concept of merit goods can be extended to include a socially desirable outcome like creation of employment. In the absence of the project, the government perhaps would be willing to pay unemployment compensation or provide mere make-work jobs.

In the case of a demerit good, the social value of the good is less than its economic value. For example, a country may regard alcoholic products as having social value less than economic value. The procedure for adjusting for the difference between social value and economic value is as follows: (i) Estimate the economic value. (ii) Calculate the adjustment factor as difference between the ratio of social value to economic value and unity. (iii) Multiply the economic value by the adjustment factor to obtain the adjustment. (iv) Add the adjustment to the net present value of the project as calculated in stage four.

LITTLE-MIRRLEES APPROACH

I.M.D. Little and J.A. Mirrlees have developed an approach (hereafter referred to as the L-M approach) to social cost benefit analysis. The LM technique assumes that a country can buy and sell any quantity of a particular good at a given world price. Hence, all traded inputs and outputs are valued at their international prices (CIF for importables and FOB for exportables) which is the opportunity cost/value of the particular good to the country. Every input is treated as a forex outgo and every   output is treated as a forex inflow. All non-tradable inputs are valued at accounting prices. These costs are broken up into tradable goods and other non-traded goods. Following this chain of production, commodities that are either exported or imported are determined for application of accounting prices. The theory assumes that non-tradables form an insignificant part of operating costs Despite considerable similarities there are certain differences between the two approaches:

1. The UNIDO approach measures costs and benefits in terms of domestic rupees whereas the L-M approach measures costs and benefits in terms of international prices, also referred to as border prices.
2. The UNIDO approach measures costs and benefits in terms of consumption whereas the Little-Mirrlees approach measures costs and benefits in terms of uncommitted social income.
3. The stage-by-stage analysis recommended by the UNIDO approach focuses on efficiency, savings and redistribution considerations in different stages. The Little-Mirlees approach, however, tends to view these considerations together.

SCBA IN INDIA

In India, SCBA of projects is carried out mainly by the Project Appraisal Division of Planning Commission and the Central financial institutions.

Project Appraisal Division

The Project Appraisal Division (PAD, hereafter) of the Planning Commission, set up in April 1972, was entrusted with the following functions:

1. To suggest standard formats for submission of projects and procedures for their techno-economic evaluation;
2. To conduct actual techno-economic evaluation of selected major projects and programmes posed to the Planning Commission;
3. To assist state government and central ministries in giving effect to standardized formats and procedures for project evaluation; and
4. To undertake and support research leading to progressive refinement of methodology and procedure of project evaluation. The Project Appraisal Division follows a modified version of the L-M methodology. In order to eliminate the trade-offs between growth (efficiency) and equity, PAD divides investments into three categories: (i) capital-intensive industrial projects, (ii) infrastructural investments, and (iii) agriculture, rural development and related projects.

The procedure followed by PAD for evaluating capital intensive industrial projects is described briefly below:

Capital Intensive Industrial Projects— Efficiency is the key criterion in the evaluation of capital intensive industrial projects which represent about 20 per cent of the total projects appraised by PAD. The methodology followed for evaluating these projects is as follows:

1. All tradeable inputs and outputs are valued at border prices.
2. Transfer cost items (taxes, duties, etc.) are ignored.
3. All non-tradeable items, especially power and transport, are evaluated in terms of marginal cost.
4. Foreign exchange involved in the inputs and outputs are valued at specified premia.
5. Saving in domestic rupees rather than foreign exchange.

Central Financial Institution

The Central financial institutions—ICICI, IFCI, and IDBI—appraise investment proposals primarily from the financial point of view. However, in recent years they have recognized the need for scrutinizing projects from the larger social point of view. ICICI was perhaps the first financial institution to introduce a system of economic analysis as distinct from financial profitability analysis. IFCI adopted a system of economic appraisal in 1979. Finally, IDBI also introduced a system for economic appraisal of projects financed by them. Though there are some minor variations, the three institutions follow essentially a similar approach which is a simplified version of the L-M approach. The appraisal procedure followed by IDBI is described below:

IDBI, in its economic appraisal of industrial projects, considers three aspects:
- Economic rate of return
- Effective rate of protection
- Domestic resource cost

Economic rate of return— The method followed by IDBI to calculate economic rate of return may be described as 'partial Little-Mirrlees' method because while international prices are used for valuation of tradeable inputs and outputs, L-M method is not followed in its entirety. The significant elements of IDBI's method are described below:

1. International prices are regarded as the relevant economic prices and, hence, it is necessary to substitute market prices with international prices for all non-labour inputs and outputs.

2. For tradeable items, where international prices are directly available, CIF prices are used for inputs and FOB prices are used for outputs.

3. For tradeable items where international prices are not directly available and for non-tradeable items (like electricity, transportation, etc.) social conversion factors are used to convert actual rupee cost into social cost. In some cases (like land) a social conversion factor is applied directly to the actual rupee cost. In other cases (like transport) the actual rupee cost is broken down into three components— tradeable component, labour component, and residual component— and these components are valued in social terms. Generally, the social cost of the tradeable component is obtained by multiplying it by a factor of 1/1.5; the social cost of labour component is obtained by multiplying it by a factor of 0.5 (shadow price of labour is considered to be 50 per cent of the actual); the social cost of the residual component is obtained by multiplying it by a factor of 0.5.

Effective rate of protection— The effective rate of protection (ERP) is calculated as follows:

$$\frac{\text{Value added at domestic prices - Value added at world prices}}{\text{Value added at world prices}} \times 100$$

Domestic resource cost— The domestic resource cost (DRC) is calculated as follows:

$$\frac{\text{Value added at domestic prices}}{\text{Value added at world prices}} \times \text{Exchange Rate}$$

PUBLIC INVESTMENT DECISION MAKING IN INDIA

The public sector has been assigned a pre-eminent role in the Indian economy. Though public investment was made in the infrastructure even before independence, the bulk of the investment in the public sector has been made after independence. The public sector today commands a predominant position in many basic industries: coal, crude oil and refining, steel, copper, basic drugs, locomotives, fertilizers, earth movers, machine tools, etc.

The public investment board (PIB) appraises and recommends the projects coming under the purview of the central government. The PIB is assisted by various agencies in its appraisal work. The criteria adopted by the PIB are as follows:

1. Conformity of the project with the priorities specified in the plan for allocation of funds.
2. Advisability of undertaking the project in the public sector or joint sector.
3. Adequacy of financial internal rate of return.
4. Adequacy of economic internal rate of return. (This is the internal rate of return of the stream of social costs and benefits.)
5. Contribution of the project to foreign exchange earnings.
6. Availability of plan funds and convenience of budgetary allocation.
7. Logical sequencing of project schedule.
8. Adequacy of safety and anti-pollution measures.
9. Soundness of marketing strategy.

UNIT IV
ANALYSIS OF PROJECT RISK, MARKET RISK AND FIRM RISK
INTRODUCTION

It is a well established fact that every project involves risk. Moreover, it is a practice to include a short summary of project risks in the project appraisal report. There are certain projects for which economic benefits can be quantified while for others, such quantification is not possible. Firm risk stem from technological change in production process, managerial inefficiency, availability of raw material, labour problems and changes in consumer preferences. The financial risk considers the difference between EBIT and EBT while business risk causes the variations between revenue and EBIT. These are ways and means to reduce the project risks.

ANALYSIS OF PROJECT RISKS

It is the normal practice to include a short summary of project risks in each appraisal report. The purpose of this chapter is to provide a summary of project risks in order to help ensure uniformity and consistency in appraisal reports. Section-1 relates to projects for which economic benefits can be quantified and section-2 deals with projects for which such quantification is not possible.

Projects with quantified benefits

The economic internal rate of return (EIRR) is the measure most often used to indicate the economic viability of financed projects. Calculation of the EIRR requires a set of assumptions regarding the conditions faced by the project which in the judgement of the appraisal mission are most likely to prevail during its life. However, since bank financed projects normally have a very long life, the conditions faced by the project may change for a variety of reasons. Sensitivity analysis is, therefore, carried out to determine the effects of possible changes in the values of key variables (costs, yields, and price of inputs and outputs) on the project's EIRR. The number of risks facing a project could be large, and it is neither possible nor desirable to identify all possible risks associated with a project. The risks discussed in the appraisal report should essentially be those which entail major economic consequences. These should be identified from the sensitivity analysis and described in descending order of importance with regard to their impact on the EIRR. Particular attention should be paid to risks that would substantially reduce the project's EIRR or render the project uneconomic by reducing its EIRR below the opportunity cost of capital. In this context, both the base-case EIRR and the sensitivity indicators are relevant. If the basecase EIRR is high, the discussion of project risks should generally include risks to which the project is highly sensitive. For example, the EIRR of most projects is highly sensitive to changes in project output, which may in turn depend on a number of factors. A discussion of the safeguards employed to minimize the risk of the outputs falling substantially below the level expected should therefore be included. For example, in an irrigation project, apart from the availability of water, output may depend on the supply of other inputs, provision of extension services, effectiveness of water management by farmer's groups, and availability of adequate infrastructure and storage facilities. Measures taken to ensure adequate and timely availability of each should be briefly explained. Risks are obviously greater in projects for which the base-case EIRR isonly marginally higher than the opportunity cost of capital. These larger risks are even greater if the EIRR is highly sensitive to changes in key variables since even a small reduction in the EIRR would render the project unviable. Even when the EIRR is relatively insensitive to changes in key variables, combinations of adverse changes might easily affect the project's viability. Thus, in such cases, the remedial action proposed or adopted should be fully explained. If the project output is traded internationally, one risk may be future changes in the price of the output, particularly if the share of a project or the country's output is small relative to the world market. In such cases, a review of world demand and supply forecasts for the good in question should be included. By their very nature, certain types of projects such as gas and oil exploration involve very high risks. For such projects, it is necessary to supplement the sensitivity analysis with a probability analysis. The latter provides a range of possible outcomes in terms of a probability distribution and based on that project related decision could be made more intelligently. But the analysis is more complex and requires more information about events affecting the project. Due to the considerable work involved,, probability analysis of risks is usually undertaken only for project carrying a high degree of risk or for large projects where miscalculations could lead to a major loss to the economy. For such projects, the nature of the risks involved and the measures taken or recommended to minimize the risks, together with the results of the analyses, should be discussed in the appraisal report.

Projects for which benefits are not quantifiable

For projects in certain sectors or sub-sectors such as education, health, sanitation and family planning, project benefits cannot be quantified and the risks cannot be measured by sensitivity analysis. In such cases, the relationship of project risks to the project's objectives should be explained. The eventualities that might impede the realization of the objectives should be discussed in relation to the project cost and output, and also in relation to the socio-economic objectives sought by the project. In such projects, the risks are greater on the benefit side than on the cost side. For instance, in education projects, school buildings and equipment are provided to help achieve a prescribed annual output of graduates with a certain skill level. However, provision of the facilities alone may not ensure achievement of the project objectives. Their achievement may depend more upon the availability of trained teachers, provision of sufficient funds for the recurring expenditures of the institutions, curriculum and admission standards, and motivation of the students. While it is not possible to eliminate all such risks, it is essential to minimize them. Major risks of this type should be identified and explained along with the remedial measures proposed in the section in which project risks are discussed. The real benefits of this type of project relate to broad socio-economic goals. For education projects, these may include increased income level for the trainees and a higher level of industrial and agricultural productive. For family planning projects, the broad goals may be an increased number of acceptors and a consequent reduction in the rate of population growth. The success of these projects depends not merely on the facilities provided, but also on the continued favourable conditions assumed by the appraisal mission. For such projects, the assumptions made regarding the relationship between the facilities provided and project's long-term objectives should be clearly explained. The conditions or facilities necessary but external to the project should also be identified, together with relevant assurances received from the government. For projects such as these, this is one of the most important aspects to be discussed in the section dealing with project risks.

MARKET RISK

The market risk affects all the projects in an industry and not a particular project. In this section, the concept of market risk has been explained with respect to factors which are beyond the control of individual corporates. The market risk is further sub-divided into:

(i) Security market risk: Often we read in the newspaper that the stock market is in the bear hug or in the bull grip. This indicates that the entire market is moving in a particular direction either downward or upward. The economic conditions, political situations and the sociological changes affect the security market. The recession in the economy affects the profit prospect of the industry and the stock market. The 1998 recession experienced by developed and developing countries has affected the stock markets all over the world. The South East Asian crisis has affected the stock market world wide. There factors are beyond the control of the corporate and the investor. They cannot be entirely avoided by the investor. It drives home the point that the market risk is unavoidable. Jack Clark Francis has defined market risk as that portion of total variability of return caused by the alternating forces of bull and bear markets. When the security index moves upward haltingly for a significant period of time, it is known as bull market. In the bull market, the index moves from a low level to the peak. Bear market is just a reverse to the bull market; the index declines haltingly from the peak to a market low point called trough for a significant period of time. During the bull and bear market more than 80 per cent of the securities' prices rise or fall along with the stock market indices. The forces that affect the stock market are tangible and intangible events. The tangible events are real events such as earthquake, war, political uncertainty and fall in the value of currency. Another example that can be cited is the Pokhran blast on May 13, 1998, and the fall of BSE sensex by 162 points. Impending sanctions, dampened sentiments and FIIs selling of stocks set a bear phase. Several examples like fall in the value of rupee and post-budget blue can be cited for triggering the bear phase. Intangible events are related to market psychology. The market psychology is affected by the real events. But reactions to the tangible events become over reactions and they push the market in a particular direction. Take for instance, the bull run in 1994 FII's investment and liberalization policies gave buoyancy to the market. The market psychology was positive. Small investors entered the market and prices of stocks without adequate supportive fundamental factors soared up. In 1996, the political turmoil and recession in the economy resulted in the fall of share prices and the small investors lost faith in the market. There was a rush to sell the shares and the stocks that were floated in the primary market were not received well. Thus, any untoward political or economic event would lead to a fall in the price of the security which would be further accentuated by the over reactions and the herd like behaviour of the investors. If some financial institutions start disposing the stocks, the fear grips in and spreads to other investors. This results in a rush to sell the stocks. The actions of the financial institutions would have a snowballing effect. This type of over reaction affects the market adversely and the prices of the scrips' fall below their intrinsic values. This is beyond the control of the corporate.

(ii) Interest rate risk: Interest rate risk is the variation in the single period rates of return caused by the fluctuations in the market interest rate. Most commonly interest rate risk affects the price of bonds, debentures and stocks. The fluctuations in the interest rates are caused by the changes in the government monetary policy and the changes that occur in the interest rates of treasury bills and the government bonds. The bonds issued by the government and quasi-government are considered to be risk free. If higher interest rates are offered, investor would like to switch his investments from private sector bonds to public sector bonds. If the government to tide over the deficit in the budget floats a new loan/bond of a higher rate of interest, there would be a definite shift in the funds from low yielding bonds to high yielding bonds and from stocks to bonds. Likewise, if the stock market is in a depressed condition, investors would like to shift their money to the bond market, to have an assured rate of return. The best example is that in April 1996, most of the initial public offerings of many companies remained under subscribed but IDBI and IFC bonds were oversubscribed. The assured rate of return attracted the investors from the stock market to the bond market. The rise of fall in the interest rate affects the cost of borrowing. When the call money market rate changes, it affects the badla rate too. Most of the stock traders trade in the stock market with the borrowed funds. The increase in the cost of margin affects the profitability of the traders. This would dampen the spirit of the speculative traders who use the borrowed funds. The fall in the demand for securities would lead to a fall in the value of the stock index. Interest rates not only affect the security traders but also the corporate bodies who carry their business with borrowed funds.

The cost of borrowing would increase and a heavy outflow of profit would take place in the form of interest t the capital borrowed. This would lead to a reduction in earnings per share and a consequent fall in the price of share.

(iii) Purchasing Power Risk: Variations in the returns are caused also by the loss of purchasing power of currency. Inflation, is the reason behind the loss of purchasing power. The level of inflation proceeds faster than the increase in capital value. Purchasing power risk is the probable loss in the purchasing power of the returns to be received. The rise in price penalizes the returns to the investor, and every potential rise in price is a risk to the investor. The inflation may be demand-pull or cost-push inflation. In the demand pull inflation, the demand for goods and services are in excess of their supply. At full employment level of factors of production, the economy would not be able to supply more goods in the short run and the demand for products pushes the price upward.d the supply cannot be increased unless there is an expansion of labour force or machinery for production. The equilibrium between demand and supply is attained at a higher price level. The cost-push inflation, as the name itself indicates that the inflation or the rise in price is caused by the increase in the cost.The increase in the cost of raw material, labour and equipment makes the cost of production high and ends in high price level. The producer tries to pass the higher cost of production to the consumer. The labourers or the working force try to make the corporate to share the increase in the cost of living by demanding higher wages. Thus, the cost push inflation has a spiraling effect on price level.

FIRM RISK

Firm risk is unique and peculiar to a firm or an industry. Firm risk stems from managerial inefficiency, technological change in the production process, availability of raw material, changes in the consumer preference, and labour problems. The nature and magnitude of the above mentioned factors differ from industry to industry, and company to company. They have to be analysed separately for each industry and firm. The changes in the consumer preference affect the consumer products like television sets, washing machine, refrigerators, etc. more than they affect the iron and steel industry. Technological changes affect the information technology industry more than that of consumer product industry. Thus, it differs from industry to industry. Financial leverage of the companies that is debt-equity portion of the companies differs from each other. The nature and mode of raising finance and paying back the loans, involve a risk element. All these factors from the firm risk and contribute a portion in the total variability of the return. Broadly, firm risk can be classified into:

1. Business risk
2. Financial risk

1. Business risk: Business risk is that portion of the firm risk caused by the operating environment of the business. Business risk arises from the inability of a firm to maintain its competitive edge and the growth or stability of the earnings. Variation that occurs in the operating environment is reflected on the operating income and expected dividends. The variation in the expected operating income indicates the business risk. For example take ABC and XYZ companies. In ABC company, operating income could grow as much as 15 per cent and as low as 7 per cent. In XYZ company, the operating income can be either 12 per cent or 9 per cent. When both the companies are compared, ABC company's business risk is higher because of its high variability in operating income compared to XYZ company. Thus, business risk is concerned with the difference between revenue and earnings before interest and tax. Business risk can be divided into external business risk and internal business risk.

(a) Internal Business Risk: Internal business risk is associated with the operational efficiency of the firm. The operational efficiency differs from company to company. The efficiency of operation is reflected on the company's achievement of its pre-set goals and the fulfillment of the promises to its investors. The various reasons of internal business risk are discussed below:

(i) Fluctuations in the sales— The sales level has to be maintained. It is common in business to lose customers abruptly because of competition. Loss of customers will lead to a loss in operational income. Hence, the company has to build a wide customer base through various distribution channels. Diversified sales force may help to tide over this problem. Big corporate bodies have long chain of distribution channel. Small firms often lack this diversified customer base.

(ii) Research and development (R&D)— Sometimes the product may go out of style or become obsolescent. It is the management, who has to overcome the problem obsolescence by concentrating on the in-house research and development program. For example, if Maruti Udyog has to survive the competition, it has to keep its Research and Development section active and introduce consumer oriented technological changes in the automobile sector. This is often carried out by introducing sleekness, seating comfort and break efficiency in their automobiles. New products have to be produced to replace the old one. Short sighted cutting of R & D budget would reduce the operational efficiency of any firm.

(iii) Personnel management— The personnel management of the company also contributes to the operational efficiency of the firm. Frequent strikes and lock outs result in loss of production and high fixed capital cost. The labour productivity also would suffer. The risk of labour management is present in all the firms. It is up to the company to solve the problems at the table level and provide adequate incentives to encourage the increase in labour productivity. Encouragement given to the labourers at the floor level would boost morale of the labour force and leads to higher productivity and less wastage of raw materials and time.

(iv) Fixed cost— The cost components also generate internal risk if the fixed cost is higher in the cost component. During the period of recession or low demand for product, the company cannot reduce the fixed cost. At the same time in the boom period also the fixed factor cannot vary immediately. Thus, the high fixed cost component in a firm would become a burden to the firm. The fixed cost component has to be kept always in a reasonable size, so that it may not affect the profitability of the company.

(v) Single product— The internal business risk is higher in the case of firm producing a single product. The fall in the demand for a single product would be fatal for the firm. Further, some products are more vulnerable to the business cycle while some products resist and grow against the tide. Hence, the company has to diversify the products if it has to face the competition and the business cycle successfully. Take for instance, Hindustan Lever Ltd., which is producing a wide range of consumer cosmetics is   thriving successfully in the business. Even in diversification, diversifying the product in the unknown path of the company may lead to an internal risk. Unwidely diversification is as dangerous as producing a single good.

(b) External risk— External risk is the result of operating conditions imposed on the firm by circumstances beyond its control. The external environments in which it operates exert some pressure on the firm. The external factors are social and regulatory factors, monetary and fiscal policies of the government, business cycle and the general economic environment within which a firm or an industry operates. A government policy that favours a particular industry could result in the rise in the stock price of the particular industry. For instance, the Indian sugar and fertilizer industry depend much on external factors. The various external factors are being discussed below:

(i) Social and regulatory factors— Harsh regulatory climate and legislation against the environmental degradation may impair the profitability of the industry. Price control, volume control, import/export control and environment control reduce the profitability of the firm. This risk is more in industries related to public utility sectors such as telecom, banking and transportation.The governments' tariff policy of the telecom sector has a direct bearing on its earnings. Likewise, the interest rates and the directions given in the lending policies affect the profitability of the banks. Calcutta Electric and Supply Company (CESC) has not been able to increase its power tariff due to the stiff resistance by the West Bengal government. The Pollution Control Board has asked to close most of the tanneries in Tamil Nadu, which has affected the leather industry.

(ii) Political risk— Political risk arises out of the change in the government policy. With a change in the ruling party, the policy also changes. When Sri. Manmohan Singh was the finance minister, liberalization policy was introduced. During the Bharathiya Janta Party government, even though efforts are taken to augment the foreign investment, more stress is given to Swadeshi. Political risk arises mainly in the case of foreign investment. The host government may change its rules and regulations regarding the foreign investment. From the past, an example can be cited. In 1977, the government decided that the multinationals must dilute their equity and share their growth with the Indian investors. This forced many multinationals to liquidate their holdings in the Indian companies.

(iii) Business cycle— The fluctuations of the business cycle lead to fluctuations in the earnings of the company. Recession in the economy leads to a drop in the output of many industries.

Steel and white consumer goods industries tend to move in tandem with the business cycle. During the boom period, there would be hectic demand for steel products and white consumer goods. But at the same time, they would be hit much during the recession period. At present, the information technology industry has resisted the business cycle and moved counter cyclically during the recession period. The effects of the business cycle vary from one company to another. Sometimes, companies with inadequate capital and consumer base may be forced to close down. In some other case, there may be a fall in the profit and the growth rate may decline. This risk factor is external to the corporate bodies and they may not be able to control it.

2. Financial risk

It refers to the variability of the income to the equity capital due to the debt capital. Financial risk in a company is associated with the capital structure of the company. Capital structure of the company consists of equity funds and borrowed funds. The presence of debt and preference capital results in a commitment of paying interest or pre fixed rate of dividend. The residual income alone would be available to the equity holders. The interest payment affects the payments that are due to the equity investors. The debt financing increases the variability of the returns to the common stock holders and affects their expectations regarding the return. The use of debt with the owned funds to increase the return to the share holders is known as financial leverage. Debt financing enables the corporate to have funds at a low cost and financial leverage to the shareholders. As long as the earnings of a company are higher than the cost of borrowed funds, shareholders' earnings are increased. At the same time when the earnings are low, it may lead to bankruptcy to equity holders. This can be illustrated with the help of the following example:

	Years		
	1996	1997	1998
Company A			
Equity capital Rs. 10 per share	20,00,000	20,00,000	20,00,000
Debt fund (10% interest)	10,00,000	10,00,000	10,00,000
Operating income	30,00,000	40,00,000	20,00,000
Earning per share	1.0	1.5	0.5
Company B			
Equity capital Rs. 10 per share	10,00,000	10,00,000	10,00,000
Debt fund (10% interest)	20,00,000	20,00,000	20,00,000
Operating income	30,00,000	40,00,000	20,00,000
Earnings per share	1.0	2.0	Nil

The above example deals with three different situations. In the year 1996, both the companies earned the same amount and the earnings per share were same. But, in the year 1997 there was 33.33 per cent hike in the earnings of the two companies. In company A 33.33 per cent rise in operating income has resulted in a 50 per cent increase in earnings per share. In the company B, earnings per share has increased by cent per cent i.e. from Rs. 1 to Rs. 2, because the bond holders receive only the fixed interest whether the company fared well or not. The increase in earnings per share would cause a change in the capital appreciation in the shares of the "B" company during a good year. In the year 1998, the economic climate has changed and there is a fall in the operating profit by 33.33 per cent for both the companies. This has caused 50 per cent fall in earnings per share for company a compared to 1996. But company "B"s earnings per share has fallen to zero and the shareholders are affected adversely in the bad year,. If we assume another situation of negative earnings, the situation would be worse in company B and the shareholders will be affected much. A few years of persistent negative earnings will erode the shareholders' equity. Fixed return on borrowed capital either enhances or reduces the return to shareholders. The financial risk considers the difference between EBIT and EBT (earnings before tax). The business risk causes the variations between revenue and EBIT. The payment of interest affects the eventual earnings of the company stock. Thus, volatility in the rates of return on the stock is magnified by the borrowed money. The variations in income caused by the borrowed funds in highly levered firms are greater compared to the companies with low leverage. The financial leverage or financial risk is an avoidable risk because it is the management who has to decide, how much to be funded with the equity capital and borrowed capital.

MULTIPLE PROJECTS AND CONSTRAINTS
INTRODUCTION

When investment projects are considered individually, any of the discounted cash flow technique may be applied for obtaining a correct accept or reject criteria. In an existing organisation, however, capital investment projects often cannot be considered individually or in isolation. This is because the pre-conditions for viewing projects individually- project independence, lack of capital rationing, and project divisibility are rarely, if ever, fulfilled. Under the constraints obtained in the real world, the so called rational criteria per se may not necessarily signal the correct decision.

CONSTRAINTS

Project Dependence : Project A and B are economically dependent if the acceptance or rejection of one changes the cash flow stream of the other or affects the acceptance or rejection of the other. The most conspicuous kind of economic dependency occurs when projects are mutually exclusive. If two or more projects are mutually exclusive, acceptance of any one project out of the set of mutually exclusive project automatically precludes the acceptance of all other projects in the set. From an economic point of view, mutually exclusive projects are substitutes for each other. For example, the alternative possible uses of a building represent a set of mutually exclusive projects. Clearly if the building is put to one use, it cannot be put to any other use. Economic dependency also exists when projects, even though not mutually exclusive, negatively influence each other's cash flows if they are accepted together. Bierman and Smidt have given an excellent illustration of this kind of economic dependency: a project for building a toll bridge and a project for operating a toll ferry. These two project are such that when they are undertaken together, the revenues of one will be negatively influenced by the other. Further, the projects are said to have positive when there is complementarity between projects. If undertaking a project influences favourably the cash flows of another project, the two projects are complementary projects. Complementarity may be of two types: asymmetric complementarity and symmetric complementarity. In asymmetric complementarity, the favourable effect extends only in one direction.

Capital Rationing: Capital rationing exists when funds available for investment are inadequate to undertake all projects which are otherwise acceptable. Capital rationing may arise because of an internal limitation or an external constraint. Internal capital rationing is caused by a decision taken by the management to set a limit to its capital expenditure outlays; or, it may be caused by a choice of hurdle rate higher than the cost of capital of the firm. Internal capital rationing, in either case, results in rejection of some investment projects which otherwise are acceptable. External capital rationing arises out of the inability of the firm to raise sufficient amounts of funds at a given cost of capital. In a perfect market, a firm can obtain all its funds requirement at a given cost of capital. In the real world, however, the firm can raiseonly a limited amount of funds at a given cost of capital. Beyond a certain point, the cost of capital tends to increase.

Project Indivisibility : Capital projects are considered indivisible, i.e. a capital project has to be accepted or rejected in toto - a project cannot be accepted partially. Given the indivisibility of capital projects and the existence of capital rationing, the need arises for comparing projects. To illustrate this point, consider an example. A firm is evaluating three projects A, B, and C which involve an outlays of Rs. 0.5 million, Rs. 0.4 million, and Rs. 0.3 million respectively. The net present value of these projects are Rs. 0.2 million, Rs. 0.15 million, Rs. 0.1 million respectively. The funds available to the firm for investment are Rs. 0.7 million. In this situation, acceptance of project A (project with the highest net present value) which yields a net present value of Rs. 0.2 million results in the rejection of projects B and C which together yield a combined net present value of Rs. 0.25 million. Hence, because of the indivisibility of projects, there is a need for the comparison of projects before the acceptance/rejection decisions are taken.

METHOD OF RANKING

Two approaches are available for determining which project to accept and which project to reject : (i) the method of ranking, and (ii) the method of mathematical programming.This section discusses the method of ranking ; the following section discusses themethod of mathematical programming. The method of ranking consists of two steps : (i) Rank all projects in a decreasing order according to their individual NPV's, IRR's or BCR's. (ii) Accept project in that order until the capital budget is exhausted. The method of ranking, originally proposed by Joel Dean is seriously impaired by two problems: (i) conflict in ranking as per discounted cash flow criteria, and (ii) project indivisibility.

Conflict in Ranking

In a given set of projects, preference ranking tends to differ from one criterion to another. For example, NPV and IRR criteria may yield different preference rankings. Likewise, there may be a discrepancy between the preference rankings of NPV and BCR (benefit cost ratio) criteria. When preference rankings differ, the set of projects selected as per one criterion tends to differ from the set of projects selected as per some other criterion. This may be illustrated by an example. Consider a set of five projects, A, B, C, D, and E, for which the investment outlay, expected annual cash flow, and project life are as shown below:

Project	Investment outlay	Expected annual cash flow	Project life
	(Rs)	(Rs)	(Years)
A	10,000	4,000	12
B	25,000	10,000	4
C	30,000	6,000	20
D	38,000	12,000	16
E	35,000	12,000	9

The NPV, IRR and BCR for the five projects and the ranking along these dimensions are shown in Exhibit below

NPV, IRR and BCR for the Five Projects

Project	NPV (Rs)	NPV Ranking	IRR (Per cent)	IRR Ranking	BCR	BCR Ranking
A	14,776	4	39	1	2.48	1
B	5,370	5	22	4	1.21	5
C	14,814	3	19	5	1.49	4
D	45,688	1	30	2	2.20	2
E	28,936	2	29	3	1.83	3

It is clear that in the above case the three criteria rank the projects differently. If there is no capital rationing, all the projects would be accepted under all the three criteria though internal ranking may differ across criteria. However, if the funds available are limited, the set of projects accepted would depend on the criterion adopted. What causes ranking conflicts? Ranking conflicts are traceable to differing assumptions made about the rate of return at which intermediate cash flows are re-invested.

Project Indivisibility

A problem in choosing the capital budget on the basis of individual ranking arises because of indivisibility of capital expenditure projects. To illustrate, consider the followingset of projects (ranked according to their NPV) being evaluated by a firm which has a capital budget constraint of Rs. 2,500, 000.

Project	Outlay	NPV
	Rs	Rs.
A	1,500,000	400,000
B	1,000,000	350,000
C	800,000	300,000
D	700,000	300,000
E	600,000	250,000

If the selection is based on individual NPV ranking, projects A and B would be included in the capital budget- these projects exhaust the capital budget. A cursory examination, however, would suggest that it is more desirable to select projectsB, C, and D. These three projects can be accommodated within the capital budget of Rs. 2,500,000, and have a combined NPV of Rs. 850,000, which is greater than the combined NPV of projects A and B.

Feasible Combinations Approach

The above example suggests that the following procedure may be used for selecting the set of investments under capital rationing.

1. Define all combinations of projects which are feasible, given the capital budget restriction and project interdependencies.

2. Choose the feasible combination that has the highest NPV.

To illustrate this procedure, consider the following projects that are being evaluated by a firm which has a capital budget constraint of Rs. 3,000,000.

Project	Outlay	NPV
	Rs.	Rs.
A	1,800,000	750,000
B	1,500,000	600,000
C	1,200,000	500,000
D	750,000	360,000
E	600,000	300,000

Projects B and C are mutually exclusive. Other projects are independent

Given the above information the feasible combinations and their NPV are shown below:

Feasible combination	Outlay	NPV
	Rs.	Rs.
A	1,800,000	750,000
B	1,500,000	600,000
C	1,200,000	500,000
D	750,000	360,000
E	600,000	300,000
A and C	3,000,000	1,250,000
A and D	2,550,000	1,110,000
A and E	2,400,000	1,050,000
B and D	2,250,000	960,000
B and E	2,100,000	900,000
C and D	1,950,000	860,000
C and E	1,800,000	800,000
B, D and E	2,850,000	1,260,000
C, D and E	2,550,000	1,160,000

The most desirable feasible combination consists of projects B, D and E as it has the highest NPV.

MATHEMATICAL PROGRAMMING APPROACH

The ranking procedure described above becomes cumbersome as the number of projects increases and as the number of years in the planning horizon increases. To cope with a problem of this kind, it is helpful to use mathematical programming models. The advantage of mathematical programming models is that they help in determining the optimal solution without explicitly evaluating all feasible combinations. A mathematical programming model is formulated in terms of two broad categories of equations: (i) the objective function, and (ii) the constraint equations. The objective function represents the goal or objective the decision maker seeks to achieve. Constraint equations represent restrictions-arising out of limitations of resources, environmental restrictions, and managerial policies-which have to be observed. The

mathematical model seeks to optimize the objective function subject to various constraints. Though a wide variety of mathematical programming models is available, but we should discuss two types:
- Linear programming model.
- Integer programming model.

LINEAR PROGRAMMING MODEL

The linear programming model is based on the following assumptions :
- The objective functions and the constraint equations are linear.
- All the coefficients in the objective function and constraint equations are defined with certainty.
- The objective function is uni dimensional.
- The decision variables are considered to be continuous.
- Resources are homogeneous. This means that if 100 hours of direct labour are available, each of these hours is equally productive.

Linear Programming Model of a Capital Rationing Problem

The general formulation of a linear programming model for a capital rationing problem is:

$$\text{Maximize} \quad \sum_{j=1}^{n} NPV_j X_j \tag{7.1}$$

$$\text{Subject to} \quad \sum_{j=1}^{n} CF_{jt} X_j \leq K_t \, (t = 0,1,\ldots,m) \tag{7.2}$$

$$0 \leq X_j \leq 1 \tag{7.3}$$

where NPVJ = net present value of projects j

   Xj = amount of projects j accepted

  CFjt = cash outflow required for project j in period t

   Kt = capital budget available in period t

The following features of the model may be noted.
1. All the input parameters-NPVJ,CFJT, Kt- are assumed to be known with certainty.
2. The Xj decision variables are assumed to be continuous but limited by a lower restriction (0) and an upper restriction (1).
3. The NPV calculation is based on a cost of capital figure which is known with certainty.

Lorie and Savage Problem

In their classic paper, "Three Problems in Rationing Capital," Lorie and Savage discussed the following nine-project, two-period problem:

Project	Net present value (NPV_j)	Cash outflow in period (CF_{j1})	Cash outflow in period (CF_{j2})
1.	14	12	3
2.	17	54	7
3.	17	6	6
4.	15	6	2
5.	40	30	35
6.	12	6	6
7.	14	48	4
8.	10	36	3
9.	12	18	3

The linear programming formulation of this problem is as follows :

Maximize $\quad 14X_1 + 17X_2 + 17X_3 + 15X_4 + 40X_5$
$\qquad\qquad + 12X_6 + 14X_7 + 10X_8 + 12X_9$

Subject to

$\qquad 12X_1 + 54X_2 + 6X_3 + 6X_4 - 30X_5 + 6X_6$
$\qquad + 48X_7 + 36X_8 + 18X_9 + S_1 \qquad = 50$ Funds constraint for year1

The linear programming formulation of this problem is as follows :

Maximize 14X1+ 17X2+ 17X3+ 15X4+ 40X5
$\qquad$ + 12X6 +14X7 +10X8 +12X9

Subject to
$\qquad$ 12X1 +54X2 +6X3 +6X4 +30X5 +6X6
$\qquad$ +48X7 +36X8 +18X9 +S1 $\qquad$ = 50 Funds constraint for year1

$\qquad$ 3X1 +7X2 +6X3 +2X4 +35X5 +6X6
$\qquad$ + 4X7 +3X8 +3X9 +S2 $\qquad$ =20 Funds constraint for year 2

X1 + S3 = 1	X4 + S6 = 1 X7 + S9 = 1	Upper limit
X1 + S3 = 1	X4 + S6 = 1 X7 + S9 = 1	Upper limit
X2 + S4= 1	X5 + S7 = 1 X8 + S10 = 1	on project
X3 + S5 = 1	X6 + S8 = 1 X9 + S11 = 1	acceptance

$$X_j \,\varepsilon\, 0 \ (j = 1,2 ,.... , 9)$$
$$S_j \,\varepsilon\, 0 \ (i = 1,2 ,.... , 11)$$

The linear programming solution for the above problem is shown in Exhibit blow . From
Exhibit below we find that

1. The basic variables (variables which take a positive value in the optimal solution) are X1,
X3, X4, X6, X7, X9, S4, S7, S8, S9, and S10. Their values are shown in the last column of the
tableau (X1 = 1.0; X3 = 1.0; X4 = 1.0; X6 = .969697, and so on).

2. The rest of the variables (X2, X5, X8, S1, S2, S3, S5, S6, and S11) are non-basic variables,

which means that they take a zero value. A value of zero for X1, X3, and X8 means that these three projects are completely rejected in the optimal solution. A value of zero for S1 and S2 implies that the budgets of 50 in year 1 and 20 in year 2 are fully exhausted on the six accepted projects.

INTEGER LINEAR PROGRAMMING MODEL

Weingartner discussed the integer linear programming approach. The principal motivation for the use of integer linear programming approach are : (i) It overcomes the problem of partial projects which besets the linear programming model because it permits only 0 or 1 value for the decision variables. (ii) It is capable of handling virtually any kind of project interdependency. The basic integer linear programming model for capital budgeting under capital rationing is as follows :

Linear Programming Formulation of Optimum Lorie-Savage Nine-Project Problem

Exhibit 7.2 ***Linear Programming Formulation of Optimum Lorie-Savage Nine-Project Problem***

Basic Variables	X_1	X_2	X_3	X_4	X_5	X_6	X_7	X_8	X_9	S_1	S_2	S_3	S_4	S_5	S_6	S_7	S_8	S_9	S_{10}	S_{11}	RHS
X_1	1.0											1.0									1.00
X			1.0											1.0							1.00
X_4				1.0											1.0						1.00
X_6		.455			5.91	1.0				-.015	.1818	-3.64			-2.73					-2.73	.96969
X_7		1.068			-.144		1.0	.75		.023	-.023	-.205		-1.0	-0.91					-.341	.04545
X_9									1.0											1.0	1.00
S_4		1.0											1.0								1.00
S_7					1.0											1.0					1.00
S_8		-.455			5.91					0.15	.1818	.364		-1.0	.273		1.0			.273	.03030
S_9		-1.068			.114			-.75		-.023	.023	.205			.091			1.0		.341	.95454
S_{10}								1.0											1.0		1.00
Z	0	3.41	0	0	29.32	0	0	.50	0	.1364	1.864	6.77	0	6.0	10.45	0	0	0		3.957	0.273
	μ_1	μ_2	μ_3	μ_4	μ_5	μ_6	μ_7	μ_8	μ_9	P_1	P_2	Y_1	Y_2	Y_3	Y_4	Y_5	Y_6	Y_7	Y_8	Y_9	

Maximize
$$\sum_{j=1}^{n} X_j NPV_j \quad (7.4)$$

Subject to
$$\sum_{j=1}^{n} CF_{jt} X_j \leq K_t (t=0,1,\ldots\ldots,m) \quad (7.5)$$

$$X_j = (0, 1) \quad (7.6)$$

It may be noted that the only difference between this integer linear programming model and the basic linear programming model discussed earlier is that the integer linear programming model ensures that a project is either completely accepted (Xj = 1) or completely rejected (Xj = 0).

Incorporating Project Interdependencies in the Model

By constraining the decision variables to 0 and 1, the integer linear programming model can handle almost any kind of project interdependency. To illustrate, let us see how the following kinds of projects interdependencies are incorporated in the integer linear programming model :

• Mutual exclusiveness

• Contingency

• Complementariness

Mutual Exclusiveness If two or more projects are mutually exclusive, acceptance of any one project out of the set of mutually exclusive projects, automatically precludes the acceptance of all other projects in the set. From an economic point of view, mutually exclusive projects are substitutes for each other. Mutual exclusiveness is reflected in the integer programming model by the following constraint :

$$\sum_{J \in J} X_j \le 1 \qquad (7.7)$$

where $\qquad$ J = the set of mutually exclusive projects under consideration

$\qquad$ $J \in J$ = an expression which means that project J belongs to set J

Constraint (7.7) means that the upper limit on the number of projects that can be selected from the set J is 1. This , of course, means that the firm may not select any project from the set J. If it is necessary to choose one project but only one project, constraint (7.11) would become :

$$\sum_{J \in J} X_j = 1 \qquad (7.8)$$

An important variant of the mutual exclusiveness condition is one in which the firm may delay a projects for one or more years. Consider, for example, projects X :

Time	Cash flow
0	–10,000
1	3,000
2	3,000
3	3,000
4	3,000
5	3,000

The NPV of this project, given a cost of capital of 12 percent, is 814. If the firm can delay this project by 1 or 2 years, two new projects X' and X" can be defined :

Time	Cash flow of X'	Cash flow of X"
0	-	-
1	-10,000	-
2	3,000	-10,000
3	3,000	3,000
4	3,000	3,000
5	3,000	3,000
6	3,000	3,000
7	-	3,000

The NPV's of projects X' and X" to be included in the objective function are respectively727 and 649. These values naturally differ from the NPV of X because of delays in cash flows associated with X' and X". Since at best only one of the projects-X, X' and X"-can be accepted, the following constraint is incorporated in the integer linear programming model :

$$X + X' + X'' \leq 1 \qquad (7.9)$$

Contingency: A contingency relationship between two or more projects implies that the acceptance of one project is contingent on the acceptance of some other project (s). For example, if project B cannot be accepted without accepting project A, we say that project B is contingent on project A. Put differently, project A is a prerequisite project for project B. Such a relationship is represented by the following constraint in the integer linear programming model.

$$X_B \leq X_A \qquad (7.10)$$

It may be noted that as per constraint (7.10), project B can be accepted only when project A is accepted; project A however, can be accepted independently. A project may be contingent on not one but two (or even more) projects. Suppose, the acceptance of project R is contingent on the acceptance of projects P and Q. Such contingency relationship is reflected in the following constraint.

$$2X_R \leq X_P + X_Q \qquad (7.11)$$

Mutual Exclusiveness and Contingency : Project dependency may reflect both mutual exclusiveness and contingency requirements. Some examples are described below :

1. P and Q are mutually exclusive projects; a third project, Z, is contingent on the acceptance of either P or Q. This condition is reflected in the following constraints:

$$X_P + X_Q \leq 1 \qquad (7.12)$$
$$X_Z \leq X_P + X_Q \qquad (7.13)$$

2. Out of the set of projects, A, B, C and D, only three projects can be accepted. Further, for accepting project E at least two projects out of the above set should be accepted. This condition is reflected in the following constraints :

$$XA + XB + XC + XD \leq 3 \qquad\qquad (7.14)$$
$$2XE \leq XA + XB + XC + XD \qquad\qquad (7.15)$$

Complementariness If undertaking a project influences favourably the cash flows of an other project, the two projects are complementary projects. To illustrate how complementarity is reflected in the integer linear programming model, consider two projects R and S. Either of them can be accepted individually. However, if both are accepted together the following benefits will accrue : (i) The cost will reduce by 5 percent. (ii) The net cash inflow will increase by 10 percent. To reflect a complementary relationship of this kind, a composite project *RS* representing the combination of R and S is set up; the cash inflows of RS would be 10 percent higher than the sum of the ncash inflows of R and S. Further, since it is not possible to accept R and S as well as RS, because the latter is the composite project consisting of R and S, the following constraint is incorporated in the integer linear programming formulation:

$$XR + XS + XRS \leq 1 \qquad\qquad (7.16)$$

Integer Linear Programming Formulation : An Illustration

Consider the following projects.

Project	Net present value (NPV_J)	Cash outflow in year 1 (CF_{J1})	Cash outflow in year 2 (CF_{J2})
1	44	50	48
2	30	40	22
3	20	10	40
4	25	36	5
5	35	25	60
6	24	43	15
7	42	40	0
8	28	33	14
9	60	75	48

The budget constraints for the two years are 150 and 180 respectively. The following project interdependencies obtain:

1. Projects 1 and 2 are mutually exclusive.
2. Out of the set of projects 4, 5, and 6 at least too must be accepted.
3. Project 9 cannot be accepted unless projects 4 and 6 are accepted.
4. Project 7 can be delayed by one year. Such a delay would not change the cash outflows but reduce NPV to 35.
5. Project 8 and 9 are complementary. If the two are accepted together, the total outflows will be less by 8 percent whereas the NPV will be more by 10 percent.

Given the nature of the problem, in addition to the decision variables X1 through X9 for the original 9 projects, few additional decision variables are required as follows:

X10 is the decision variable to represent the delay of project 7 by one year.

X11 is the decision variable for the composite project which represents the combination of projects 8 and 9.

The integer linear programming formulation is as follows:

Maximize $44X1 + 30X2 + 20X3 + 25X4 + 35X5 + 24X6 + 42X7 + 28X8 + 60X9 + 35X10 + 96.8X11$

Subject to

$$50X1 + 40X2 + 10X3 + 36X4 + 25X5 + 43X6 + 40X7 + 33X8 + 75X9 + 0X10 + 99.4X11 \leq 150$$

$$48X1 + 22X2 + 40X3 + 5X4 + 60X5 + 15X6 + 0X7 + 14X8 + 48X9 + 40X10 + 47.88X11 \leq 180$$

$$X1 + X2 \leq 1$$

$$2X9 \leq X4 + X6$$

$$X7 + X10 \leq 1$$

$$X8 + X9 + X11 \leq 1$$

$$Xj = \{0,1\}\ j = 1, 2, \ldots., 11$$

Evaluation

The merits of the integer linear programming model are :

1. It overcomes the problem of partial projects which besets the linear programming model.
2. It is capable of handling virtually any kind of project interdependency.

The main limitations of the integer linear programming model are :

1. The solution of linear programming model takes considerably more time than the solution of the integer of the linear programming model. Pettway reported that for an integer linear programming model with 28 projects and 15 budget constraints, four out of six algorithms that he tried failed to reach an optimal solution in 5 minutes in CPU time on an IBM 360-65 system; the two algorithms which located the optimal solution took 118 seconds and 181 seconds. By contrast, the solution time for the linear programming model of the same problem would take just one to two seconds.

2. Meaningful shadow prices are not available for the integer programming formulation. This happens because the integer linear programming model permits only discrete variation, not continuous variation, of the decision variable. In the integer linear programming model, constraints which are not binding in the optimal solution are assigned zero shadow prices though the objective function would decrease when the availability of resources representing non-binding constraints, is diminished.

.

NETWORK TECHNIQUES FOR PROJECTMANAGEMENT

INTRODUCTION

Projects are successful if they are completed on time, within budget, and to performance requirements. Management of any project involves planning, coordination and control of a number of interrelated activities with limited resources, namely men, machines,money and time. Furthermore, it becomes necessary to incorporate any change from the initial plan as they occur, and immediately know the effects of the change. Thereforethe managers are compelled to look for and depend on a dynamic planning and schedule system which will not only produce the best possible initial plan and schedule, but will also sufficiently dynamic to

react instantaneously to changed in the original plan and schedule. The question of such a dynamic system/ technique led to the development of *network analysis.* It provides a framework which :
> defines the job to be done,
> integrates them in a logical time sequence and finally,
> affords a system of dynamic control over the progress of the plan.

Network analysis is a generic name for a number of associated project planning and control procedures that are all based on the concept of network. PERT, an acronym for Program Evaluation and Review Technique and CPM, an acronym for Critical Path Method are the two widely used techniques of project management that were developed, independently and simultaneously, during the 1950s. The network analysis underlying PERT and CPM helps to support the three phases of effective project management.

Planning
> identify the distinct activities,
> determine their durations and interdependencies,
> construct a network diagram,
> determine minimum overall project duration (using the network diagram), and
> identify the tasks critical (i.e. essential) to this minimum duration.

Scheduling
> construct schedule ('time chart'),
> schedule contains start and finish times for each activity, and
> evaluate cost-time trade-offs (evaluate effects of putting extra money, people or machines in a particular task in order to shorten project duration).

Controlling
> monitor/control project by use of network diagram,
> follow progress of the various activities ; and
> make adjustment where appropriate.

PERT/CPM : BACKGROUND and DEVELOPMENT

PERT and CPM- both techniques use similar network models and methods are have the same general purpose. They were developed during the late 1950s. PERT was originally developed by the U S Navy's Special Product Office in cooperation with the consulting firm of Booz, Allen and Hamilton. It was developed as a network flow chart to facilitate the planning and scheduling of the Polaris Fleet Ballistic Missile Project, a massive project with about 250 contractors and about 9000 sub contractors and its application is credited with saving two years from the original of five years required to complete the project. Designed to handle risk and uncertainty, PERT is eminently suitable for research and development and programmes, aerospace projects, and other projects involving new technology. In such projects the time required for completing various jobs or activities can be highly variable. Hence the orientation of PERT is 'probabilistic'.

CPM, is akin to PERT. It was developed (Independently) in 1956-57 by the Du Pont Company in the US to solve scheduling problems in industrial settings. CPM is primarily concerned with the trade-off between cost and time. It has been applied mostly to projects that employ fairly stable technology and are relatively risk free. Hence its orientation is 'deterministic'. As both PERT and CPM approaches to Project Management use similar network models and methods, the term PERT and CPM are sometimes used interchangeably or collectively as PERT-CPM methods. The differences between those tools come from how they treat the activity time. PERT treats activity time as a random variable whereas CPM requires a single deterministic time value for each activity. Another difference is that PERT focuses exclusively on the time variable whereas CPM includes the analysis of the time/Cost trade-off.

The PERT/CPM is capable of giving answers to the following questions to the project manager :

- ➤ when will the project be finished ?
- ➤ when is each individual part of the scheduled to start and finish ?
- ➤ of the numerous jobs in the project, which one must be timed to avoid being late ?
- ➤ is it possible to shift resources to critical jobs of the project from other non-critical jobs of the project without affecting the overall completion time of the project ?
- ➤ among all the jobs in the project, where should management concentrate its efforts at one time ?

Methodologically, PERT/CPM were developed from traditional GANTT Charts used for scheduling and reviewing the progress of activities. Developed by Harry Gantt in 1916, these charts give a time line for each activity. They are used for planning, scheduling and then recording progress against these schedules. Basically there are two basic types of Gantt Charts : Load Charts and Project Planning Charts.

Load Charts : This type of chart is useful for manufacturing projects during peak or heavy load periods. The format of the Gantt Load Chart is very similar to the Gantt Project Planning Chart, but, Load Chart, uses time as well as departments, machines or employees that have been scheduled.

Project Planning Chart

It addresses the time of individual work elements giving a time line for each activity of a project. This type of chart is the predecessor of the PERT. As it can be seen in the Figure, it is really easy to understand the graph, but in developing it you need to take into consideration certain precedence relationship between the different activities of the project. On the chart, everyone is able to see when each activity start and finishes but there is no possibility to determine when each activity may start or if we can start a particular activity before finishing the immediate predecessor activity. Therefore, we need somehow know the precedence relationship between activities. This is the main reason for using the PERT/CPM tools instead of using exclusively Gantt Charts. Widely diverse kind of projects can be analyzed by the techniques of PERT/CPM. In fact they are suitable for any situation where :

(a) the project consists of well-defined collection of activities or tasks.

(b) the activities can be started and terminated independently of each other, even if the resources employed on the various activities are not independent.

(c) the activities are ordered so that they can be performed in a technological sequence. Thus precedence relationships exist which preclude the start of certain activities until other are completed. For instance, road leveling cannot start unless the roadbed is laid. We now proceed to discuss the techniques to provide answers to the types of questions stated earlier. The initial step in each of these is to portray the given project graphically by means of network, which provide the basic tool for analysis.

DEVELOPMENT OF PROJECT NETWORK

Basic to network analysis is the networks diagram. Both the methods of PERT and CPM graphic representation of a project that it is called "Project Network" or "Project Diagram" or "CPM

Diagram", and it is used to portray graphically the interrelationships of the elements of a project and to show the order in which the activities must be performed. A simple network chart for a 'Seminar Planning Project' is shown in Figure as an example.

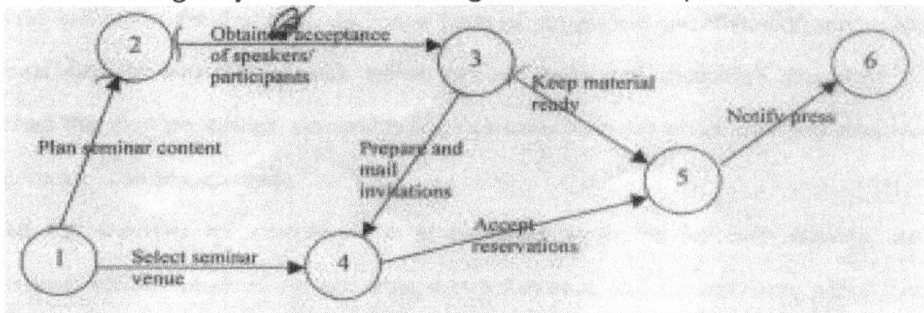

Project Network

In order to represent a project network, two basic elements are used :

A circle called **"node"**, represents an event. An event describes a checkpoint. It does not symbolize the performance of work, bit it represents the point in time in which the event is accomplished.

An arrow, called **"arc"**, represents an activity-a recognizable part of the project involving mental or physical work and requiring time and resources for its completion. The network will try to reflect all the relationships between the activities. Since activities are the basic building blocks of a network diagram, it is necessary to enumerate all the activities of the project. For this purpose, it is helpful to break theproject in several steps. The number of steps, of course, would depend on the magnitude and complexity of the project. For industrial projects generally a two-step procedure would suffice. In the first step, the major parts of the project are identified and in the second step the activities of each major part are delineated. Activities should be so defined that they are distinct, reasonably homogeneous tasks for which time and resources requirement can be estimated.

Once the activities are enumerated it is necessary to define for each activity, the activities, which precede it, the activities which follow it, and the activities which can take place concurrently. Given this information, the network diagram, showing the logical relationship between activities and events may be developed following either the forward method or the backward method. The forward method begins with the initial events, marking the beginning of the project, and proceeds forward till the end event is reached. The backward method begins with the end event and works backwards till the beginning event is reached.

Rules for constructing a project network :

Three simple rules govern the construction of a project network :

1)Each activity must be represented by only one directed arc or arrow.

2) No two activities can begin and end on the same two nodes circle. A situation like the one shown in the following figure is not permissible.

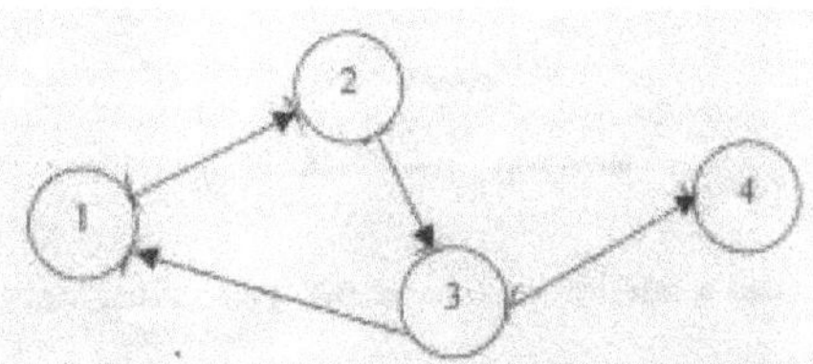

3) There should be no loops in the network. A situation like the one shown in the figure given below is not permissible.

Another element to represent a project network is a *"dummy activity"*.
Tasks that must be completed in sequence but that don't require resources or completion time are considered to have event dependency. These are represented by dotted lines with arrows and are called dummy activities. To explain it, we will consider the following example :

ACTIVITY	IMMEDIATE PREDECESSOR
A	....
B	....
C	A, B
D	B

The temptation is to represent these relationships as :

But then we have broken the second earlier mentioned. To show that activities A and B precede C, whereas activity B precedes activity D, we use a dummy activity as shown in the following figure.

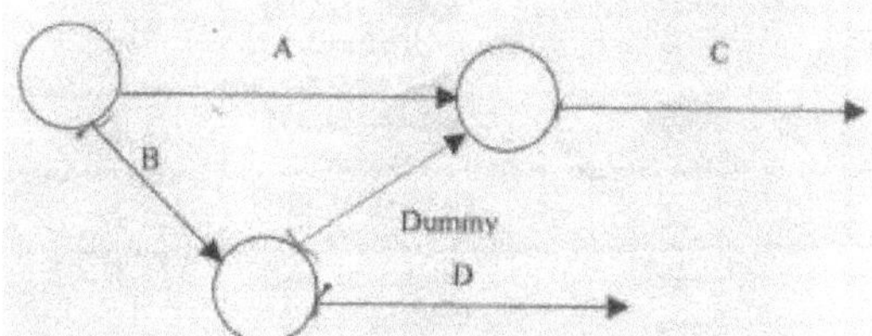

A dummy activity may also be used to represent a constraint necessary to show the proper relation ship between activities. As shown in the following figure, activities A and B must be completed before activity C can be start, only activity B must be completed before activity D can start.

To construct a project network, first of all, we need a list of activities, showing the precedence relationships between the different activities involved is shown in Table as an example.

Activities of the Project 'Launching a New Product'

ACTIVITY	NAME	IMMEDIATE PREDECESSOR	DURATION (months)
A	Market analysis	....	1
B	Product Design	A	3
C	Manufacturing study	A	1
D	Select best product design	B, C	1
E	Detailed marketing plans	D	1
F	Manufacturing process	D	3
G	Detailed project design	D	3
H	Test prototype	G	1
I	Finalize product design	F, H	1.5
J	Order components	I	1
K	Order production equipment	I	3
L	Install production equipment	K	2

Figure shows the network with the Earliest Start time, Earliest Finish time, Latest Start time and Latest Finish time of the activities (these will be discussed later in the lesson).

Because each activity must have a unique pair of starting and ending nodes, we must use a dummy activity to draw the first four activities, as shown in the figure. Constructing a project network is a trial-and-error process. It usually takes two or three attempts to produce a neatly constructed network.

Figure Network of the Project 'Launching a New Product'

TIME ANALYSIS

Once the logic and details of the project network have been established, time estimates must be assigned to each activity. With this representation we can determine the minimum completion time for the project i.e. the critical path and the critical activities and the slack or float of other activities, so that we can find the activity schedule i.e. when each activity should start and when it may be completed. For discussing these aspects of network analysis we will use the simple project shown in Figure below.

Time Estimation

Assigning time to individual activities is essential in order to analyze a network. Therefore an estimate must next be made how long each activity will take for its completion. This is done by discussing with the people responsible for the completion of the specific activities. In CPM analysis the activity time estimates are deterministic i.e. time of various activities are known so we have only one time for each activity. A distinguishing feature of PERT is its ability to deal with uncertainty in activity completion times. For each activity, the model usually includes three times estimates:

Optimistic time (a) - generally the shortest time in which the activity can be completed under ideal, favorable conditions. It is common practice to specify optimistic times to be three standard deviations from the mean so that there is approximately a 1% chance that the activity will be completed within the optimistic time.

Most likely time (m) - the completion time under the normal conditions, having the highest probability. Note that this time is different from the expected time.

Network with Three Time Estimates (in weeks)

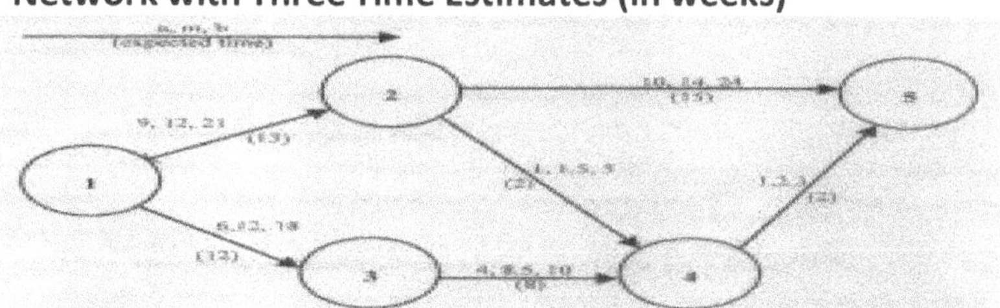

Pessimistic time (b) - the longest time under worst, externally unfavorable conditions, which an activity might require. Three standard deviations from the mean is commonly used for the pessimistic time.PERT assumes a beta probability distribution for the time estimates. For a beta distribution, the expected time for each activity can be approximated using the following weighted average :

Expected time = (Optimistic + 4 x Most likely + Pessimistic) / 6

te=(a+4m+b)/6

This expected time might be displayed on the network diagram as shown in Figure above

Determination of Critical Path

Once the network diagram with single time estimates has been developed, the following computational procedure may be employed for determining the critical path/s, event slacks, and activity floats.

Calculate the Earliest Occurrence Time (EOT) for each Event.

The EOT of an event refers to the time when the event can be completed at the earliest. Looking at event we find that the since the paths leading to it, viz, (1-2-4) and (1-3-4) take 15 weeks and 20 weeks, respectively, the EOT of event 4 is 20 weeks. In general terms, the EOT of an event is the duration of the longest path (from the beginning event whose EOT is set at 0) leading to that event. The EOTs of various events in our illustrative project are shown in Figure below It may be noted that in Figure below a circle represents an event. The upper half of the circle denotes the event number, the left quarter in the lower half denotes the EOT, and the right quarter in the lower half denotes the Latest Occurrence Time, (LOT) a term described the later. The EOT of the end event obviously represents the minimum time required for completing the project. To obtain the EOT of various events we start from the beginning event and move forward towards the end event. This computational procedure is referred to as the *forward pass.* In this computation we assume that each activity starts immediately on the occurrence of the event preceding it. Hence the starting and finishing time for various activities obtained from this computation are the Earliest Starting Time (EST) and the Earliest Finishing Time (EFT). The general formula for EOT is :

EOT (i) = Max [Eot(k) + d(k-i)]

where EOT (i) = earliest occurrence time of event i

EOT (k)=earliest occurrence time of event k (k precedes i

and there may be several k's)

d (k-i) = duration of activity (k-i)

The maximisation shown is done considering all activities (k-i) leading to event node i have been completed. The formulae for EST and EFT are :

EST (i-j) = EOT (i)

EFT (i-j) = EST (i-j)+d(i-j)

where EST (i-j) = earliest starting time for activity (i-j)

EOT (i) = earliest occurrence time of event (i)

EFT (i-j) = earliest finishing time for activity (i-j)

d(i-j) = duration of activity (i-j)

Calculate the Latest Occurrence Time (LOT) for each Event.

The LOT for an event represents the latest allowable time by which the event can occur, given the time that is allowed for the completion of the project (occurrence of end event). Normally the time allowed for the completion of the project is set equal to the EOT of the end event (In other words, the project is supposed to be completed at the earliest possible time). This means that for the end event the LOT and EOT are set equal. The LOT for various events is obtained by working backward for the end event. This procedure is known as the *backward pass*. The LOT for event 4 in our illustrative project, for example, is equal to the LOT for event 5, the end event, minus the duration of the activity (4-5), which connects event 4 with 5. Since the LOT for event 5 is 28 weeks and duration of activity (4-5) is 2 week the LOT for event 4 is 26 weeks (28-2). This represents the latest time by which event 4 should occur to enable the project to be completed in 28 weeks. Likewise, the LOT for other events can be calculated by moving backward. The LOT for various events is shown (in the right quarter of the lower half of event nodes) in Figure below:

Figure Network with EOT and LOT of Events

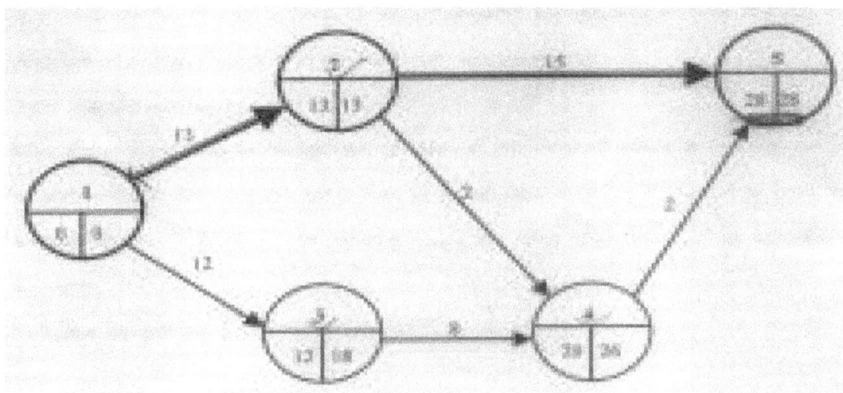

The general formula for LOT is :

LOT(i) = Min [LOT(i) - d(i-j)]

  where LOT(i) = latest occurrence time of event i

    LOT(i) = latest occurrence time of event j (ij follows i & there

      may be several j's)

   d(i-j) = duration of activity (i-j).

The minimization shown here is done with respect to all activities (i-j) starting from i Given the LOT for various events we can calculate the Latest Finishing Time (LFT) and Latest Starting Time (LST) for various activities The formulae for LFT and LST are :

LFT (i-j) = LOT (i)

LST (i-j) = LFT (i-j) -d (i-j)

  where LFT (i-j) = latest finishing time for activity (i-j)

    LOT (j) = latest occurrence time of event (j)

    LST (i-j) = latest starting time for activity (i-j)

     d (i-j) = duration of activity (i-j)

Calculate the Slack for each Event

The slack for an event is the difference between its LOT and EOT. The slacks for various events of our illustrative project are shown in Table below

Event Slack

Event	LOT	EOT	Slack = LOT - EOT
1	0	0	0
2	13	13	0
3	18	12	6
4	26	20	6
5	28	28	0

Obtain the Critical and Slack Paths

A path is a sequence of activities that leads from the starting node to the finishing node. The critical path parts with the beginning event, terminates with the end event, and is marked by events, which have a zero slack. This is obviously the path on which here is no slack, no cushion. Other paths are slack paths with some cushion. The critical path for our illustrative project is (1-2-5).

	Table 8.3	Critical and Slack Paths	
Path	**Activities**	**Duration**	**Path Slack**
1-2-4-5	1-2, 2-4, 4-5	17	28 - 17 = 11
1-3-4-5	1-3, 3-4, 4-5	22	28-22 = 6
1-2-5	1-2, 2-5	28	0

Figure Critical Path in the Network

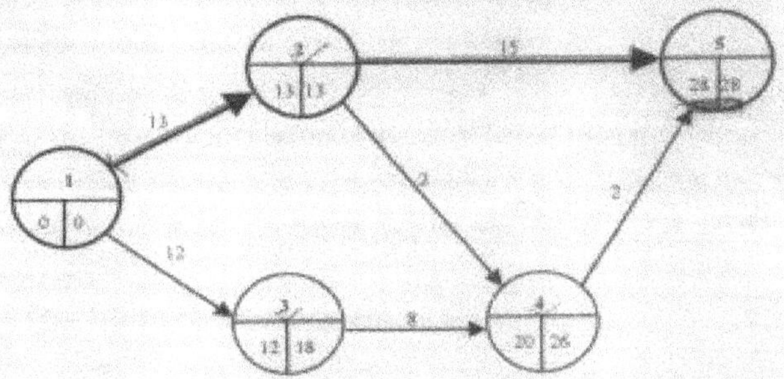

The critical path is the longest path from the beginning event to the end event. Since the end can be reached, i.e., project completed, only when this longest path is traversed, the minimum time required for completing the project is the duration on the critical path. The duration on

the critical path of our project is 28 weeks; this is the minimum time required completing the project. (It is already indicated by the EOT of event 5, the end event.)

Calculate the Activity Floats

Activity float analysis provides the information on the margin on allowance available for the commencement and completion of various activities. Activities with zero slack value represent activities on the critical path. Three types of activities floats are identified:

- ➢ Total float
- ➢ Free float
- ➢ Independent float

Total Float : Total float usually referred to as simply float or slack, is the amount of time an activity can be delayed beyond its earliest possible starting time without delaying the project completion, if other activities take their estimated duration.

Total float for activity (i-j) = LOT(i) - EOT(i) - d(i-j)

Free Float : Free float is the amount of time on the basis of which an activity can be delayed without delaying the early start of a successor activity. To find free float, we subtract the early finish of an activity from the early start times of its succeeding activities.

Free float for activity (i-j) = EOT(i) - EOT(i) - d(i-j)

Independent Float : This indicates the time span by which the activity (i-j) can be expanded or shifted if, for the event (i) the LOT and for the event (j) the EOT shall be maintained. A shifting of activity in this area has no influence on the further progress of the project. Independent float is taken as zero is negative.

Independent float for activity (i-j) = EOT(i) - LOT(i) - d(i-j)

The floats of various activities of our illustrative project are shown in Table below:

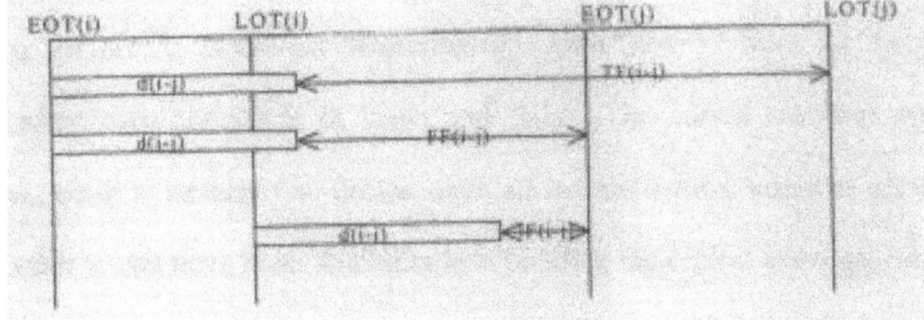

Table Activities Floats

Activity	Duration	EST	EFT	LST	LFT	Total	Free	Independent
1-2	13	0	13	0	13	0	0	0
1-3	12	0	12	6	18	6	0	0
2-4	2	13	15	24	26	11	5	5
3-4	8	12	20	18	26	6	0	-6 i.e. 0
2-5	15	13	28	13	28	0	0	0
4-5	2	20	22	26	28	6	6	0

Scheduling

Scheduling the project is the act of producing a time-table of work for the project showing when each activity os to begin and finish. The critical activities schedule themselves, but it is necessary to decide when all the non-critical activities are to take place. In other words there is no flexibility in scheduling the critical activities, but floats available with non-critical activities provide flexibility in scheduling them. The choice available in this respect is bounded by two schedules: Early Start Schedule and Late Start Schedule

Early Start Schedule

The early start schedule refers to the schedule in which all activities start as possible. In this schedule

- ➢ all events occur at their earliest because all activities start at their earliest starting time and finish at their earliest finishing time;

Figure Early Start Schedule

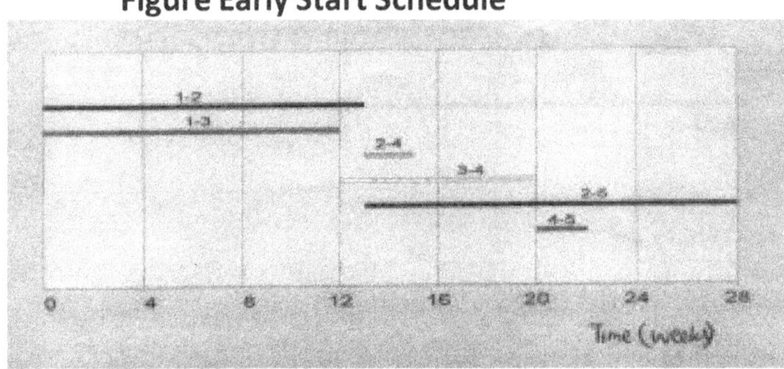

- ➢ there may be time legs between the completion of certain activities and the occurrence of events which these activities lead to; and
- ➢ all activities emanating from an event begin at the same time.

The early start schedule suggests a caution attitude towards the project and a desire to minimize the possibility of delay. It provides a greater measure of protection against uncertainties and adverse circumstances. Such a schedule, however, calls for an earlier application of resources.

Late Start Schedule

The late start schedule refers to the schedule arrived at when all activities started as late as possible. In this schedule

- ➢ all events occur at their latest because all activities start at their latest finishing time;
- ➢ some activities may start after a time lag subsequent to the occurrence of the preceding events; and
- ➢ all activities leading to an event are completed at the same time.

Figure Late Start Schedule

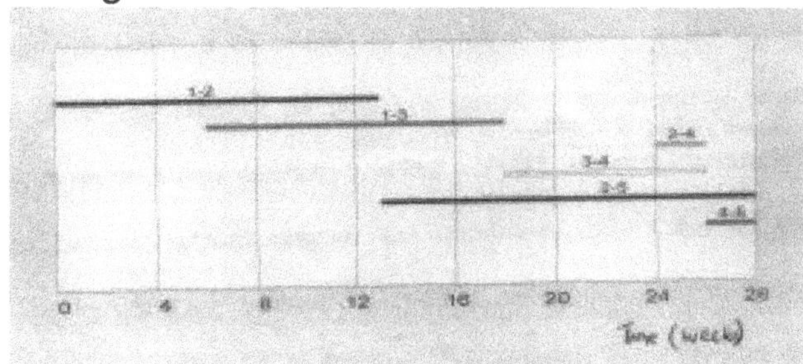

The late start schedule reflects a desire to commit resources late-as late as possible. However, such a schedule provides no elbow room in the wake of adverse developments. Any anticipated delay results in increased project duration. The early start schedule and the late start schedule for our illustrative project are shown in Figures above respectively. Here the project schedules are shown as graphs with a horizontal time scale.

PERT Analysis Variability in Time Estimates :

So far, we have discussed the procedure for determining the project completion time, the earliest and latest times for the start and completion of activities and the occurrence of events. In CPM analysis, activity duration are assumed to be known where as, in PERT, the activity duration is given by probability distributions. PERT calculates the expected duration of an activity as a weighted average of the three time estimates-optimistic (a), most likely (m) and pessimistic (b) The PERT network provides a measure of the probability of completing the project by the scheduled date. The probability concept is only associated with PERT and not CPM, because, the activity time estimates in CPM are deterministic (i.e. known) and not probabilistic. In PERT, the assessment of uncertainty for the entire network i.e. the probability of occurrences of the end event of the project is related to the degree of uncertainty - associated with the three time estimates *a,m* and *b*. PERT is almost identical to CPM to regard to its function, network diagram and calculations, except that the method of estimating activities times are different i.e., in CPM, an activity duration is based on a single time estimate, whereas, there are three time estimates made for each activity in PERT, which is converted into one time estimate

$$(i.e., expected\ time\ te) \text{ using the formula } te = (a+4m+b)/6$$

Variability in PERT analysis is measured by standard deviation or its square, variance. The variance in the project completion time can be calculated by summing the variances in the completion of the time activities in the critical path. Given the expected time and the variance, one can calculate the probability that the project will be completed by a certain time assuming a normal probability distribution for the critical path. The normal distribution assumption holds if the number of activities in the path in large enough for the central limit theorem to be applied.

Figure Normal Distribution of Critical Path Duration

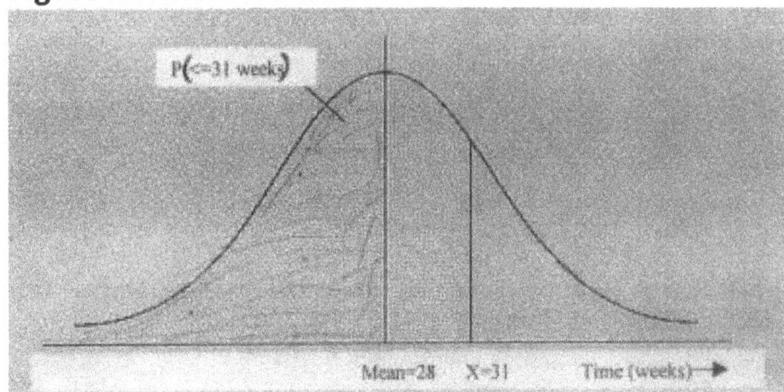

Variance and Standard Deviation of activities :

To calculate the variance for each activity completion time, if three standard deviation times were selected for the optimistic and pessimistic times, then there are six standard deviations between them, so

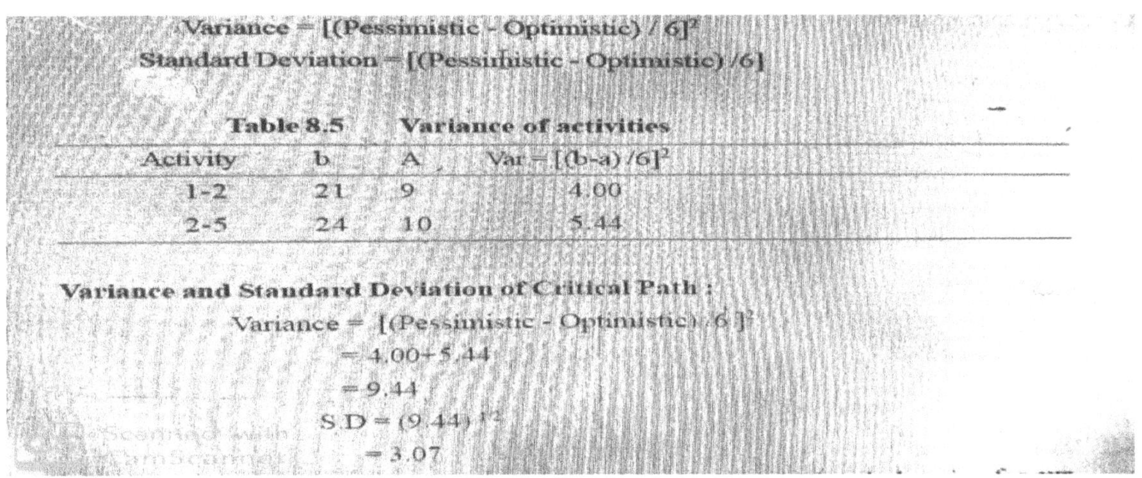

Variance = [(Pessimistic - Optimistic) / 6]²
Standard Deviation = [(Pessimistic - Optimistic) /6]

Table 8.5   Variance of activities

Activity	b	A	Var = [(b-a) /6]²
1-2	21	9	4.00
2-5	24	10	5.44

Variance and Standard Deviation of Critical Path :

Variance = [(Pessimistic - Optimistic) /6]²
= 4.00+5.44
= 9.44
S.D = (9.44)^½
= 3.07

Now we know that mean and standard deviation of the critical path duration for our project are 28 and 3.07 weeks, respectively. Given this information, we can calculate the probability that the project will be completed by a certain date.

Probability of Completion by a Specified Date

- ➢ Convert our specific normal distribution into standard normal distribution (with mean and standard deviation equal to 0 and 1 restrictively) i.e. Find z= (X- mean)/s.d.
- ➢ Obtain cumulative probablity up to z looking at the probability distribution of the standard normal variate (see Figure above)

Example 1: Find the probability of completing the project by 31 weeks

Solution : Z = (31-28)/3.07
= 0.97
Required   probability
(P<=31 weeks)= 0.8340

Example 2 : Find the probability of completing the project by 20 weeks

Solution Z = (20-28)/3.07
= -2.6
Required probability (P<=20 weeks) = 0.0197

RESOURCE ANALYSIS AND ALLOCATION

In our discussion on the scheduling of activities in determining the scheduling timings, we have considered only the technological restriction, which lay that an activity in a project can not start unless all its predecessors have been scheduled and ignored the question of resource required the performing various activities. Now we will consider the question of resource requirement for different activities, the availability of resources and their allocation.

Scheduling in view of Resource Constraints

In real life situations, there may be restrictions on the availability of resource. For example, manpower supply may be limited or funds made available period wise may be rigidly budgeted. When restrictions exist various schedules may have to be considered to find out which one is most appropriate in the light of these restrictions. We shall discuss two example to indicate the broad approach to scheduling in the face of resource constraints.

Example 1: Scheduling to Match Availability of Manpower

Let us consider a small project for which the network diagram is shown in Figure below In this project network, activity duration is shown above the activity arrow and manpower requirement is shown below the activity arrow.

Figure Network with Manpower Requirement of Activities

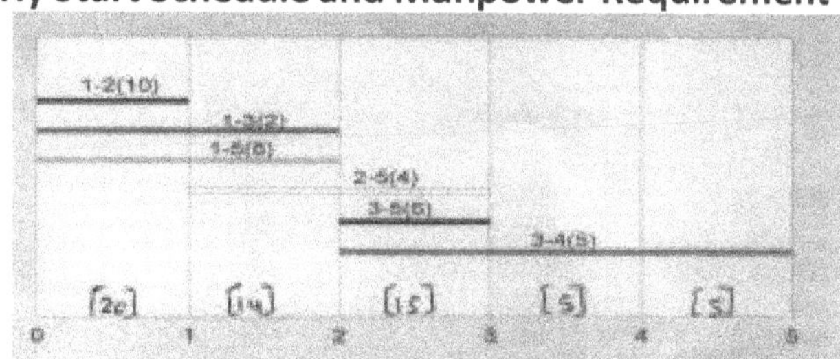

Only 12 men are available for the project (a manpower resource constraint). The early start schedule of this project is shown in Figure below .Looking at the manpower requirement for the early start schedule we find that it is 20 for the first day, 14 for the second day, 5 for the fourth day, and 5 for the fifth day. Obviously, this schedule is unacceptable in view of the manpower constraint. So, we explore the possibility of shifting activities. Our efforts of shifting activities, keeping the project duration at five days, soon reveals that no schedule is feasible with only 12 men.

Figure Early Start Schedule and Manpower Requirement

So we extend the duration of the project by one day and try various schedules to see whether we can find a feasible schedule. A little juggling of activities shown that a schedule like one shown in Figure below is feasible-this is the best we can do.

Figure Schedule to Match Manpower Supply

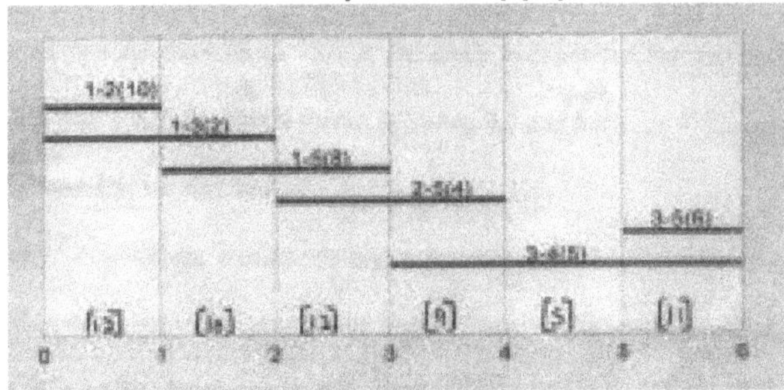

Example 2 : Scheduling to Match the Release of Funds

The cost estimates for various activities of our illustrative project are given in Table below

Table Cost Estimates of Activities

Activity	Duration	Cost per week	Total cost
1-2	13	2,000	26,000
1-3	12	5,000	60,000
2-4	2	10,000	20,000
3-4	8	2,500	20,000
2-5	15	1,000	15,000
4-5	2	7,500	15,000
Total Cost			156,000

The Management has decided to release Rs 156,000 required for the project, in the following manner : Rs 69,000 in the first 12 weeks; Rs 68,000 in the next 12 weeks, and Rs 19,000 in the 12 weeks. It has also stipulated that the unspent amount would lapse and hence cannot be carried forward. Before we develop the project schedule, a preliminary question may be asked: Is it possible *prima facie* to schedule this project without extending its duration beyond 28 weeks, which is the minimum time required given the network logic and activity duration? To answer question let us look at the funds requirement for the early start schedule and late start schedule. As shown in Tables below

From the tables, we find that :

➢ The rate of expenditure is relatively higher for the earlier stages in the early start schedule and is relatively higher for the later stages in the late start schedule.

➢ A rate of spending greater than that of the early start schedule is not possible. (This is so because in the early start schedule all activities start as early as possible.) Any release of funds above the early start schedule requirement curve is beyond the capacity of the project to spend.

Table   Funds Requirements for ESS

Weeks	Activities	Funds Required	Cumulative Total
1-12	1-2, 1-3	7*12	84
13	1-2, 3-4	4.5*1	88.5
14-15	2-4, 3-4, 2-5	13.5*5	115.5
16-20	3-4, 2-5	8.5*2	150
21-22	2-5, 4-5	1*1	151
23	2-5, 4-5	1*1	152
25-27	2-5	1*3	155
28	2-5	1*1	156

Table   Funds Requirements for LSS

Weeks	Activities	Funds Required	Cumulative Total
1-6	1-2,	2*6	12
1-12	1-2,1-3	7*6	54
13	1-2,1-3	7*1	61
14-18	1-3,2-5	6*5	91
19-24	3-4,2-5	3.5*6	112
25-26	2-4,3-4,2-5	13.5*2	139
27-28	2-5,4-5	8.5*2	156

> The rate of spending corresponding to the late start schedule is the absolute minimum necessary to complete the project on time. If the rate of spending is less than that corresponding to the late start schedule the project duration will have to be necessarily extended.

> A pattern of funds release lying between the two buouds, early start schedule requirements and late start schedule requirement, *'prima facie'* suggests that a schedule can be worked out without extending project duration.

Let us now look at the cumulative funds release pattern for our illustrative project. This lies between the early start schedule requirement and late start requirement. So *'prima facie'* it suggests that a feasible schedule without extending the project duration can be developed. Let us proceed further and consider scheduling to match the release of funds. The activities that begin in first 12 weeks, according to the early start schedule are (1-2) and (1-3). If both these activities are commenced as early as possible, the fund requirement for this period would be Rs 84,000. Since this amount exceeds Rs 69,000 (the amount to be released in first 12 weeks), the expenditure in this period has to be reduced by Rs 15,000. For this we consider the possibility of shifting activities to subsequent periods. Looking at activities (1-2) and (1-3) we find that (1-2) is on the critical path, so there is no flexibility available with respect to it. Activity (1-3), however, can be shifted, as it is not on the critical path. Since activity (1-3) requires Rs 5,000 per week, it has to be shifted by three weeks so that the amount spent in first 12 weeks is equal to the amount released in first 12 weeks. Since there is a free float of six weeks for activity (1-3), we shift it by three weeks. We now go to the next period of 12 weeks. The effects of shifting activity (1-3) by three weeks are as follows.

(a) The funds requirement for the next period of 12 weeks on account of activity (1-3) increases by Rs 15,000 over and above what it is for the early start schedule.

(b) The earliest starting time for activity (3-4) moves to 15 weeks from 12 weeks and the earliest finishing time moves to 23 weeks from 20 weeks. Since this shift.

Table   **Funds Requirements for our Proposed Schedule**

Weeks	Activities	Funds Required	Cumulative Total
1-3	1-2	2*3	6
4-12	1-2,1-3	7*9	69
13	1-2,1-3	7*1	76
14-15	1-3,2-4,2-5	16*2	108
16-23	3-4,2-5	3.5*8	136
24	2-5	1	137
25-26	2-5,4-5	8.5*2	154
27-28	2-5	1*2	156

occurs within the second period of 12 weeks, there is no change in funds requirement on account of activity (3-4). (c) The earliest starting time for activity (4-5) moves to 23 weeks from 20 weeks and the earliest finishing time for activity (4-5) moves to 25 weeks from 23 weeks. This decreases the fund requirement for the second period of 12 weeks by the Rs 7,500. The net effect, therefore, is to increase funds requirement funds by Rs 7,500 over and above what it is for the earliest start schedule. Hence the total requirement becomes Rs 68,000+Rs 7,500 = Rs 75,500. However, the funds budgeted for the second period of 12 weeks are only Rs 68,000. So we consider the possibility of shifting some activities to the third period of 12 weeks. We find that by shifting activity (4-5) to the third period of 12 weeks the expenditure in the second period of 12 weeks can be reduced to Rs 68,000, the budget of that period. As a result of this shifting the expenditure for the third period of 12 weeks (first four weeks of it) equals the budgeted funds release for this period. The schedule arrived at finally is shown in Figure blow

Figure Schedule to Match Release of funds

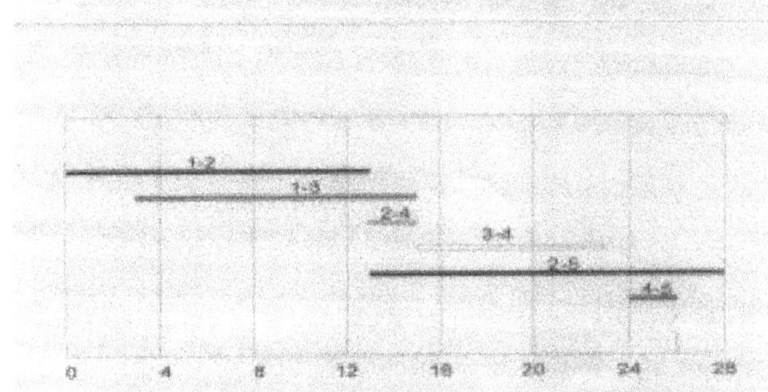

Problems in Scheduling Real Life Projects

In the above discussion we have considered simple examples comprising few activities and one constraints, to indicate the broad approach. In real life projects the activities run into hundreds and there may be several constraints. The problem of scheduling in such cases tends to become very complex. For solving such problems the technique of linear programming can be used. However, when a problem has numerous activities, say, more than 100, the technique of linear programming becomes computationally unwieldy and inordinately expensive, even with the aid of fastest computer available. In view of the practical difficulties in using linear programming for solving large scale scheduling problems, heuristic programs have been developed. A heuristic is a rule of thumb like 'schedule critical activities first or schedule the activity which has the largest independent float in the end'. A heuristic program consists of a collection of such heuristic. In recent years many heuristic programs have been developed- they are formulated usually as computer programs. These programs may be broadly divided into two types : resource levelling programs and resource allocation programs. A resource - leveling programs seeks to resource requirements, given a constraint on project duration. A resource allocation program tries to find the shortest project schedule, given fixed resource availabilities.

Project Crashing and Time-Cost Trade-offs: CPM Analysis
The project manager is confronted with having to reduce the scheduled completion time of a project to meet a deadline. Project duration can often be reduced by assigning more labor to project activities, in the form of over time, and by assigning more resources, such as material, equipment, etc. However, the additional labor and resources increase the project cost. So, the decision to reduce the project duration must be base on analysis of the trade-off between time and cost. *'Project crashing'* is a method for shortening the project duration by reducing the time of one or more of the critical project activities to less than its normal activity time. Crashing may become necessary because of many reasons, such as

- ➤ to reduce the scheduled completion time to reap the results of the project sooner.
- ➤ as project continuous over time, the team consumes indirect costs.
- ➤ there may be direct financial penalties for nor completing a project on time.

The goal of crashing is to reduce project duration at minimum cost. To reduce project duration while minimizing the cost of crashing, the project them should estimate normal time, normal cost, crash time, crash cost for each activities. And then the team can estimate total crash time, total crash cost, the crash cost per time unit to reduce project duration at minimum cost.

Assumptions underlying CPM analysis are :

1. The cost associated with a project can be divided into two components: direct cost and indirect cost. Direct cost are incurred on direct material and direct labor. Indirect costs consists of overhead items like indirect supplies, rent, insurance, managerial services etc.

2. Activities of the project can be expedited by crashing which involves employing more resources.

3. Crashing reduces time but enhances direct cost because of factors like overtime payments, extra payments, and wastage. Project crashing cost and indirect costs have an inverse relationship; crashing costs are highest when the project is shortened, whereas indirect costs increase as the project duration increase. So, the project time is at the minimum point on the total cost curve as below :

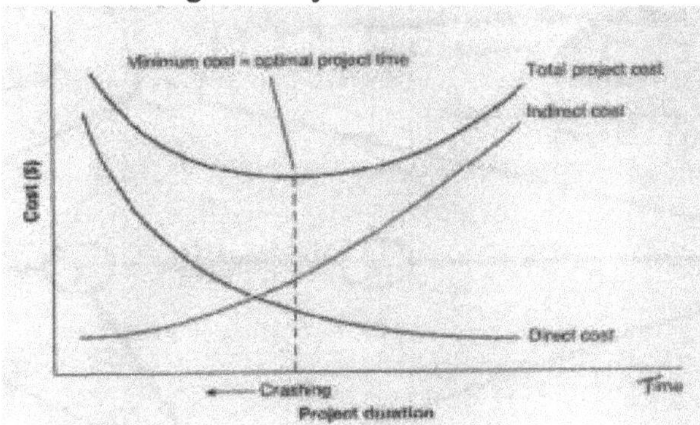

Figure Project Costs

The Time-Cost trade-off analysis comprises the following steps.

Step 1 The first step is to identify and crash the critical activity that has the minimum incremental cost of crashing. In the event of multiple critical paths, an activity from each such path is chosen. Of the various combinations available, the one with the least cost is selected. In particular, it may be economical to consider joint critical activities activities that are common to two or more critical paths. In each case, the crashing is done for one time unit-by a day if the activities times are given is days.

Step 2 In the second step, the network is revised by adjusting the time and the cost of the crashed activity. The critical path (s) is identified again, and we revert to the step1. This process is continued till no more crashing of the project is possible. Now the optimal duration of the project can be determined. It would be the time duration corresponding to which the total cost-direct cost plus indirect cost-is the minimum.

Let us consider the following example.

**Figure Network with Normal Time, Crash Time
and Crashing Cost per day of activities duration.**

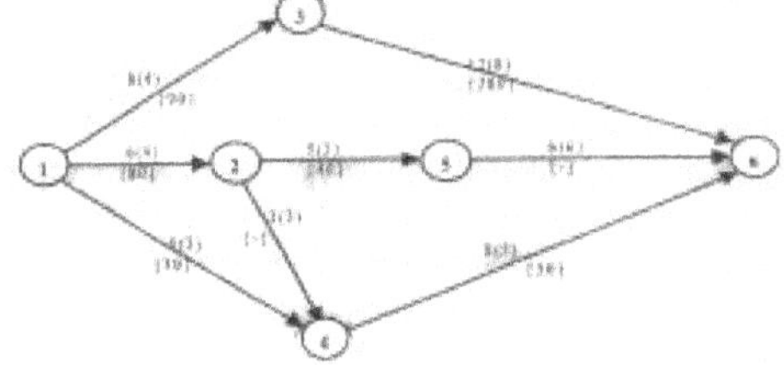

Example : The network diagram in Figure 8.14 shows for each activity need to completes the project the normal time, the shortest time in which the activity can be completed of a building contract and the cost per day for reducing the time of each activity. The contract includes a penalty clause of Rs 100 per day over 17 days. The overhead cost per day is Rs 160. The cost of completing the eight activities in normal time is Rs 6,500.

  (a) Calculate the normal duration of the project, its cost and the critical path.
  (b) Calculate and plot on a graph the cost/time function for the project and state:
      (i) the lowest cost and the associated time.
      (ii) the shortest time and associated cost.

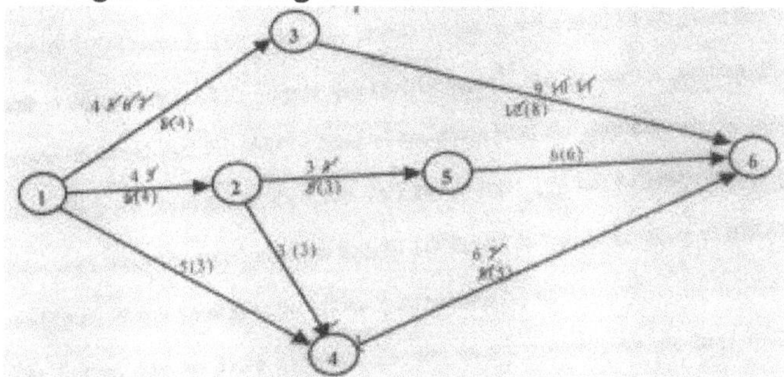

Figure Crashing of Activities

From the network, we can determine the normal project duration by the length of the critical path using normal activity time. The length of the critical path based of the crash times as shown here gives the minimum duration of the project :

Path	Normal Length	Crash Length
1-3-6	20 (critical)	12
1-4-6	13	8
1-2-4-6	17	12
1-2-5-6	17	13 (critical)

Accordingly, we have the normal and the minimum duration of the project equal to 20 and 13 days respectively. Now we shall consider the time-cost relationship for this project when it is crashed successively by a period of one day, to know the total cost of the project for durations of 20 days through 13 days.

The First Crashing : In this example, the critical activities are 1-3 and 3-6 for which the cost of reduction per day is Rs 90 and Rs 200. Obviously, we would decide to crash the activity 1-3. Crashing it by a day, the project length is reduced to 19 days and the total cost is equal to Rs 9,380. This is depicted in Table below. For the normal duration of the project it would cost Rs 10,000.(equal to the direct cost, the overhead and the penalty cost, which are, respectively, Rs 6,500; Rs 3,200(= 160 x 20); and Rs 300(= 100 x 3)). Now we change the duration of the activity 1-3 from 8 to 7 days, as shown in Figure above At this stage also, the critical path remains 1-3-6.

The second and the Third crashing : For the second crashing, we are faced with the same activities to choose from as in the first crashing, viz. 1-3 and 3-6. The situation is the same in the third crashing. The total project cost equals Rs 9,660 and Rs 9,490 after the second and the third crashing. Notice that the crashing cost at any given stage is equal to the cumulative cost of crashing till that point. After the third crashing, the critical paths, each with a length of 17 days, are : 1-3-6; 1-2-4-6; and 1-2-5-6.

The Fourth Crashing : To reduce the project length from 17 days to 16, an activity from each of these paths should be chosen. The various alternatives, along with their cost are as follows :

Alternative	Activities	Total Crashing Cost
1	1-3,1-2	90+80 = 170
2	1-3, 4-6, 2-5	90+50+40 = 180
3	3-6,1-2	200+80 = 280
4	3-6, 4-6, 2-5	200+50+40 = 290

Thus we would crash activities 1-3 and 1-2 at a cost of Rs 170. The total cost of the project at this stage is Rs 9,500, and the critical paths, after adjusting the activity timings, are the same as above.

The Fifth Crashing : For reducing the length of the project time to 15 days, we have the following alternatives. Notice that the activity 1-3 cannot be crashe any more.

Alternative	Activities	Total Crashing Cost
1	3-6, 1-2	200+80 = 280
2	3-6, 4-6, 2-5	200+50+40 = 290

Now we decide to crash activities 3-6 and 1-2 by a day each, at the additional cost of Rs 280. The project cost now equals Rs 9,620, the critical paths still being 1-3-6; 1-2- 4-5 and 1-2-5-6.

The Sixth and the Seventh Crashing : At each of these crashings, the only choice open is to crash each of the following activities-one activity from every path at a cost of Rs 290: 3-6, 4-6 and 2-5. The total cost of the project is Rs 9,750 and Rs 9,880, respectively, after these crashings. From the table 8.10, it is clear that the lowest cost is Rs 9,490 corresponding to the project duration equal to 17 days, whereas the shortest time to complete the project is 13 days at a total cost of Rs 9,880.

Table: Determination of Time-cost Relationship

Project Duration (days)	Direct Cost (Rs)				Indirect Cost (Rs)			(Rs)
	Normal	Crashing	Total	Overhead	Penalty		Total	
20	6500	-	6500	3200	300		3500	10000
19	6500	90	6590	3040	200		3240	9830
18	6500	180	6680	2880	100		2980	9660
17	6500	270	6770	2720	-		2720	9490
16	6500	440	6940	2560	-		2560	9500
15	6500	720	7220	2400	-		2400	9620
14	6500	1010	7510	2240	-		2240	9750
13	6500	1300	7800	2080	-		2080	9880

The time-cost function is shown graphically in Figure 8.16

Figure Time-Cost Function for the Project

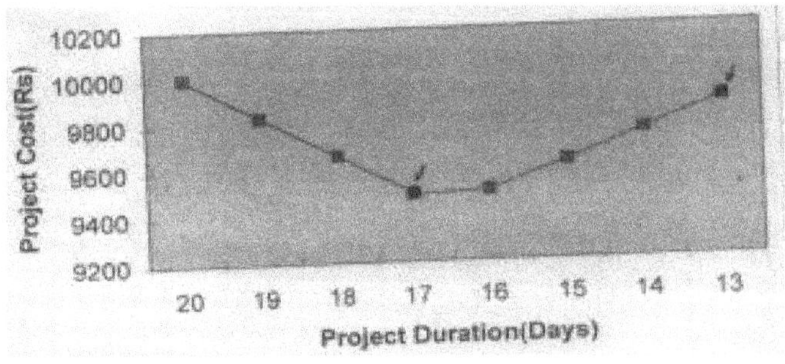

Preparation Of Project Report:
Project formulation divides the process of project development into eight distinct and sequential stages.

These stages are:
  1. *General Information.*
  2. *Project Description.*
  3. *Market Potential.*
  4. *Capital Costs and Sources of Finance.*
  5. *Assessment of Working Capital Requirements.*
  6. *Other Financial Aspects.*
  7. *Economic and Social Variables.*
  8. *Project Implementation.*
The nature of information to be collected under each one of these stages has been given below:

1. General Information:

The information of general nature given in the project report includes the following: Bio-data of Promoter: Name and address of entrepreneur; the qualifications, experience and other capabilities of the entrepreneur; if these are partners, state these characteristics of all the partners individually.

Industry Profile: A reference of analysis of industry to which the project belongs, e.g., past performance, present status, its organisation, its problems, etc.

Constitution and Organisation: The constitution and organisational structure of the enterprise, in case of partnership firm, its registration with the Registrar of Firms; application for getting Registration Certificate from the Directorate of Industries/District Industry Centre, etc.

Product Details: Product utility, product range; product design; advantages to be offered by the product over its substitutes, if any.

2. Project Description: A brief description of the project covering the following aspects is given in the project report.

Site: Location of enterprise; owned or leasehold land; industrial area; No Objection Certificate (NOC) from the Municipal Authorities if the enterprise location falls in the residential area.

Physical Infrastructure: Availability of the following items of infrastructure should be mentioned in the project report:

(i) Raw Material: Requirement of raw material, whether inland or imported, sources of raw material supply.
(ii) Skilled Labour: Availability of skilled labour in the area, arrangements for training labourers in various skills.
Utilities: These include:(i) Power: Requirement for power, load sanctioned availability of power.
(ii) Fuel: Requirement for fuel items such as coal, coke, oil or gas, state of their availability.
(iii) Water: The sources and quality of water required should be clearly stated in the project report.

Pollution Control: The aspects like scope of dumps, sewage system and sewage treatment plant should be clearly stated in case of industries producing emissions.

Communication System: Availability of communication facilities, e.g., telephone, telexes etc. should be stated in the project report.

Transport Facilities: Requirements for transport, mode of transport, potential means of transport, distances to be covered, bottlenecks etc., should be stated in the business plan.

Other Common Facilities: Availability of common facilities like machine shops, welding shops and electrical repair shops etc. should be stated in the report.

Production Process: A mention should be made for process involved in production and period of conversion from raw material into finished goods.

Machinery and Equipment: A complete list of items of machinery and equipment's required indicating their size, type, cost and sources of their supply should be enclosed with the project report.

Capacity of the Plant: The installed licensed capacity of the plant along with the shifts should also be mentioned in the project report.

Technology Selected: The selection of technology, arrangements made for acquiring it should be mentioned in the business plan.

Research and Development: A mention should be made in the project report regarding proposed research and development activities to be undertaken in future.

3. Market Potential: While preparing a project report, the following aspects relating to market potential of the product should be stated in the report:

(i) Demand and Supply Position: State the total expected demand for the product and present supply position. This should also be mentioned how much of the gap will be filled up by the proposed unit.

(ii) Expected Price: An expected price of the product to be realised should be mentioned in the project report.

(iii) Marketing Strategy: Arrangements made for selling the product should be clearly stated in the project report.

(iv) After-Sales Service: Depending upon the nature of the product, provisions made for after-sales service should normally be stated in the project report.

(v) Transportation: Requirement for transportation means indicating whether public transport or entrepreneur's own transport should be mentioned in the project report.

4. Capital Costs and Sources of Finance: An estimate of the various components of capital items like land and buildings, plant and machinery, installation costs, preliminary expenses, margin for working capital should be given in the project report. The present probable sources of finance should also be stated in the project report. The sources should indicate the owner's funds together with funds raised from financial institutions and banks.

5. Assessment of Working Capital Requirements: The requirement for working capital and its sources of supply should be carefully and clearly mentioned in the business plan or project report. It is always better to prepare working capital requirements in the prescribed formats designed by limits of requirement. It will minimise objections from the banker's side.

6. Other Financial Aspects: In order to adjudge the profitability of the project to be set up, a projected Profit and Loss Account indicating likely sales revenue, cost of production, allied cost and profit should be prepared. A projected Balance Sheet and Cash Flow Statement should also be prepared to indicate the financial position and requirements at various stages of the project.

In addition to above, the Break-Even Analysis should also be presented in the project report. Break-even point is the level of production/ sales where the industrial enterprise shall earn neither profit nor incur loss. In fact, it will just break even. Break-even level indicates the gestation period and the likely moratorium required for repayment of loans.

Break-even point (BEP) is calculated as follows:
$$BEP = F/S-V \times 100$$
$$\text{where, } F = \text{Fixed Cost}$$
$$S = \text{Sales Projected}$$
$$V = \text{Variable Costs}$$
Thus, the break-even point so calculated will indicate at what percentage of sales, the enterprise will break even i.e., no profit, no loss.

7. Economic and Social Variables: In view of the social responsibility of business, the abatement costs, i.e., the costs for controlling the environmental damage should be stated in the project. Arrangements made for treating the effluents and emissions should also be mentioned in the report.

Besides, the socio-economic benefits expected to accrue from the project should also be stated in the report itself.

Following are the examples of socio•economic benefits:

(i) Employment Generation.
(ii) Import Substitution.
(iii) Ancillarisation.
(iv) Exports.
(v) Local Resource Utilization.
(vi) Development of the Area.

8. Project Implementation: Last but no means the least, every entrepreneur should draw an implementation scheme or a time-table for his project to ensure the timely completion of all activities involved in setting-up an enterprise. Timely implementation is important because if there is a delay, it causes, among other things, a project cost overrun.

Following is a simplified implementation schedule for a small business project:

An Illustrative Implementation Schedule

Tasks / Months	1	2	3	4	5	6	7	8	9	10	11	12	13	14
1. Formulation of Project Report														
2. Application for Term-Loan														
3. Term-Loan Sanction														
4. Possession of Land														
5. Construction of Building														
6. Getting Power and Water														
7. Placing Order for Machinery														
8. Receipt and Installation of Machinery														
9. Manpower Recruitment														
10. Trial Production														
11. Commencement of Commercial Production														

The above schedule can be broken up into scores of specific tasks involved in setting up the enterprise. "Project Evaluation and Review Technique (PERT)' and "Critical Path Method (CPM)' can also be used to get better insights into all activities related to implementation of the project.